A Non-Violent Approach to Stage Violence

J. D. Martinez

illustrated by Caren Caraway

Burnham Inc., Publishers

J. D. Martinez, a graduate of the Royal Academy of Dramatic Art in London, BRA Illinois Wesleyan University, is an associate professor of theater at Washington and Lee University, Lexington, Virginia. He is a professional stage-fight director, a Certified Fight Master, and current president of the Society of American Fight Directors.

Library of Congress Cataloging-in-Publication Data

Martinez, J. D., 1949–
    Combat mime.

    Includes index.
    1. Stage fighting.   I. Title.
PN2071.P5M3   792'.028   82-3578
ISBN 0-88229-730-9 (cloth)   AACR2
ISBN 0-88229-809-7 (paper)

Manufactured in the United States of America.

10 9 8 7 6 5 4

 The paper used in this book meets the minimum requirements of American National Standard for Information Sciences—Permanence of Paper for Printed Library Materials, ANSI Z39.48-1984.

COMBAT MIME

COMBAT MIME

Contents

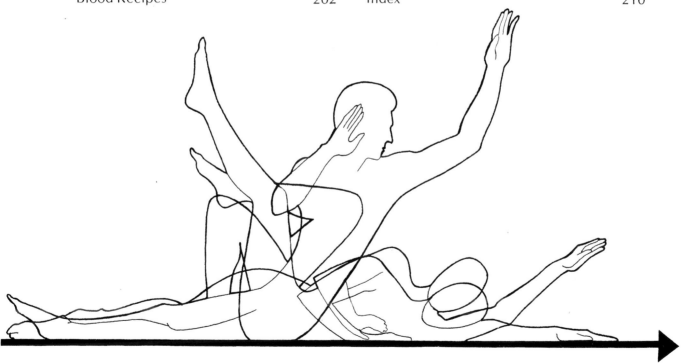

Acknowledgments

To my Father and Mother
whose peaceful home
fostered the values
of non-violence.

ALL CREATIVE PURSUITS in the performing arts are dependent on the collective efforts of a large number of people, my work reflects that dependence. I am deeply indebted to the many students, actors, and directors who have selflessly shared their insights and creative energy with me.

To my illustrator, Caren Caraway, and to my editor, Carol Gorski, I extend a respectful thank you.

I am very grateful to Alison Schmitz, whose gentle perseverance supported the work whenever my resolve weakened.

To Henry Marshall, B.H. Barry, Marvin Nelson, Hugh Cruttwell, Drew Fracher, Liam O'Brien, Reid Gilbert, Erik Fredrickson, David Boushey, Patrick Crean, Gary Boeck, and Stuart Gordon, I acknowledge an especial gratitude.

Introduction

THIS BOOK OUTLINES — in simple terms and illustrations — how to safely create the illusions of unarmed stage violence. Other fight choreographers may find in it a technique or two that is new to them and instructive, but my primary concern is for the actor, director, or stage manager who is a novice at stage violence. I sincerely hope that this simple book will help prevent injuries related to stage fights.

Each technique outlined here can be executed in an infinite number of ways, for there are literally hundreds of styles of hand-to-hand combat in existence today, as well as many varied theatrical styles. However, if the reader pays particular attention to the general principles, the techniques can safely and effectively be adapted to include other movements that suit the actor and the action.

Each technique is presented so as to lead the combatants step-by-step to the safe completion of the illusion. Don't fall into the trap of attempting to perform a technique too soon. Improvising during performance is dangerous. It is essential that both partners can rely on the constancy of movement and timing established during rehearsals.

Also essential to safety is physical preparedness through preliminary exercise.

In combat mime, as in many other physical activities, the warm-up period is important in safeguarding against strains, sprains, etc. In addition, a warm-up enhances kinesthetic awareness and aids concentration. The brain needs a plentiful supply of blood, fully oxygenated by a warmly functioning respiratory system, to be completely alert. And although a session in combat mime training, properly controlled, is relatively safe, a lack of concentration or fuzzy physical awareness could lead to injury.

For safe and progressive combat mime sessions, it is essential to maintain an open and constructive forum for criticism. In this way partners can help each other hone reflexive actions, improve timing, and thereby develop a mutual accuracy in gesture. Partners also have the responsibility of measuring the amount of force and velocity utilized during any given technique. As rapport develops, they become attuned to moments of confusion, or loss of control. As a reward for this careful cooperation, the partners eventually experience complete trust and relaxation while sharing in the exhilaration of performing a stage fight that astounds their audience.

The disciplines of combat mime also lead to growth in other areas of acting — for example, breath control, relaxation, balance, concentration, and a sense of immediacy. The myriad parallels between the art forms of combat mime and acting will become more apparent through practice of the techniques and through the experience of actual stage fights.

Finally, there are a few practical considerations. Be sure you have adequate space, sufficient lighting, a soft surface to fall on, soft-soled tennis shoes or bare feet, nonrestrictive clothing, and *no jewelry or sharp objects* of any kind on your person before you begin. If you wear glasses and cannot work without them, get a band to keep them on your head. If contact lenses will be used during a performance, wear them for practice to see if you'll have trouble with them.

That's enough for now — let's go!

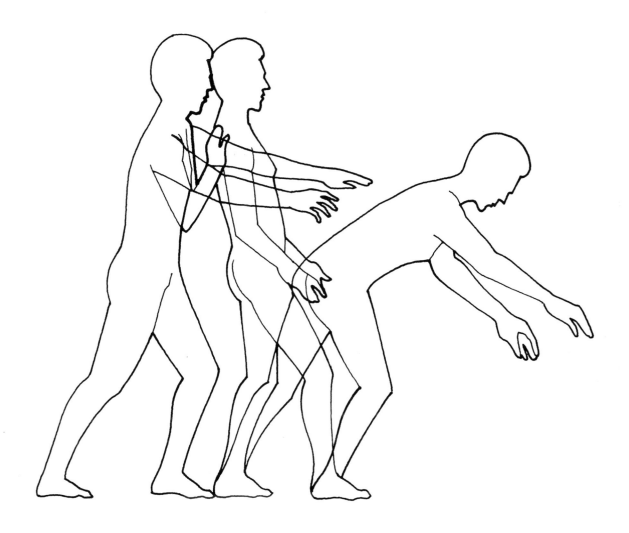

Preparatory Partner Games

*Where there is no fight,
there is no blame*

THESE GAMES ARE designed to heighten the combatants' awareness of each other. They will aid in the development of reflexes, balance, breath control, control of speed and force, and sensitivity to rapid changes in your own balance and your partner's.

I recommend that the preparatory partner games be played for a few minutes following a warm-up and prior to practicing techniques, choreographing a fight, or rehearsing a fight.

Take all your jewelry off, and get the hair out of your eyes before engaging in any combat mime technique — whether in rehearsal, out on the lawn, or in the hall demonstrating with a friend. Be extremely aware of your fingernails. They are indeed deadly weapons and they should be cut short and filed smooth before the first class. Long nails not only are dangerous to a partner, but they prevent one from forming a correct fist for punches and stand a good chance of being torn during falling and throwing techniques.

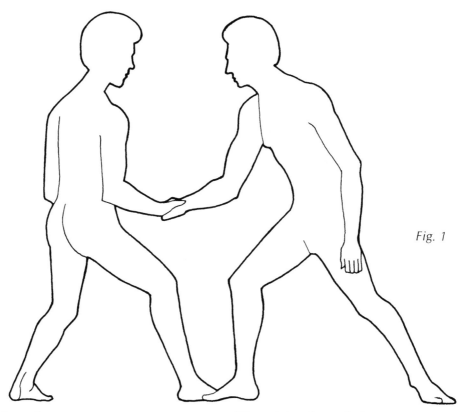

Fig. 1

Tightrope Wrestle

This game is particularly good for developing a sensitivity to your partner's changes of balance as well as involving your own center of gravity in an active way. Being aware of your partner's changes of weight distribution is crucial to many continuous contact techniques such as choking or pulling hair.

Stand facing one another with the outsides of your right feet together. Grasp right hands as in a handshake (see Figure 1). Your feet must remain stationary, as if you are balancing on a tightrope.

The objective of the game is to upset your partner's balance and either move one foot, fall to the side, or touch the ground with the free hand.

Rather than force your partner off balance through brute strength, it is better to be sensitive to your partner's changes of weight distribution so as to take advantage of a moment of imbalance.

Try playing this game with the left hands clasped and the left feet touching. Also try it with both partners' eyes closed. Playing the game "blind" increases one's ability to detect weight shifts through hand contact.

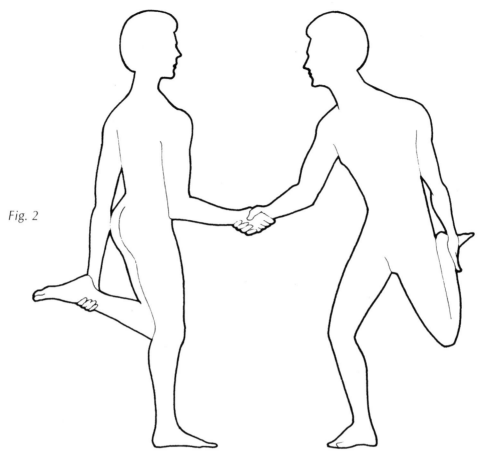

Fig. 2

Heron Wrestle

This game is a useful preliminary to practicing kicking techniques. It is a more difficult version of the Tightrope Wrestle, requiring a greater sense of balance and better control at the knees.

Grasp right hands as in a handshake, and balance on the right foot, and grasp your left ankle with your left hand (see Figure 2).

The object of the game is to cause your partner to lose balance and either move the supporting foot or fall to the side, without yourself losing balance or shifting your supporting foot. Resist the urge to "sacrifice" your own balance in an effort to imbalance your partner, as this is a more subtle game than the Tightrope Wrestle.

Try the game balancing on your left foot, or with eyes closed to heighten sensitivities.

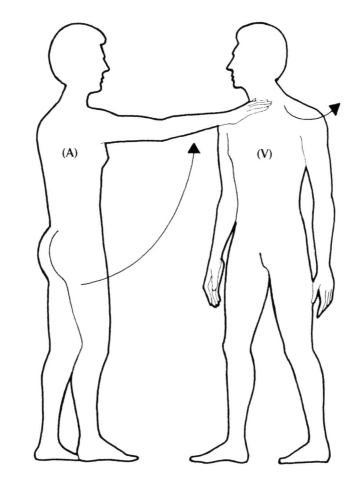

Fig. 3

Shoulder Tag

This game focuses on acquiring speed with control, and it develops reflexive reactions. Shoulder Tag requires a good deal of concentration and relaxation.

Who will be the attacker *(A)* and who the victim *(V)* should be determined before the action begins. Stand opposite each other an arm's length apart, with right feet leading, knees slightly bent, and arms hanging from the shoulders. Partners maintain eye contact throughout the game.

The object of the game is for the attacker to touch the victim's shoulder with a fingertip without bending forward from the waist. The victim must simultaneously attempt to avoid being touched by rotating the shoulder away from the attacker (see Figure 3). Neither player's feet may move.

Remember to breathe during the game, for there is a tendency to hold the breath for the sake of alertness. This is counterproductive to a relaxed readiness, which is an essential state for combat mime.

The attacker should strive for the fastest possible movement in reaching for the victim's shoulder. However, don't telegraph your intentions by tensing just prior to reaching. It's best to relax completely and wait until the need to touch your partner's shoulder builds within you, so that you're reaching forward before you've made the conscious decision to do so. In this way you surprise yourself and begin to discover those deeper reflexive responses that are very fast, direct, and relaxed.

Hand Trap

Here's another reflex game to help partners become attuned to one another very quickly. Predetermine who will be the attacker (A) and who the victim (V).

The attacker stands with the right foot leading, arms outstretched in front of the body. The victim stands with the right foot leading and with the right arm extended so that the right hand is between the hands of the attacker (see Figure 4).

The object of the game is simply for the attacker to trap the extended hand of the victim before the victim can move it out of the way — either up or down. Neither partner's feet may move.

Again we're interested in speed without force. Lightness and control are our aim.

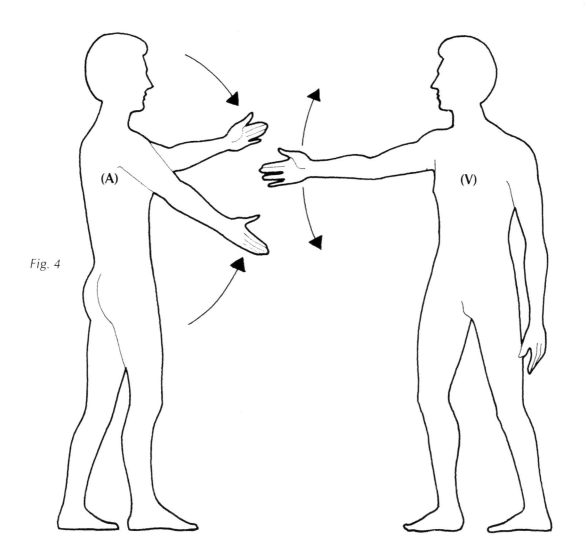

Fig. 4

Remember to keep your shoulders relaxed and to breathe. Don't be lured into false starts, either. The point is not to trick your partner, but to develop speed and reflexive reaction time.

Quick Draw

Here's another variation of the basic Hand Trap game.

The partner who is the attacker *(A)* stands with the right foot leading, arms relaxed by the sides. The victim *(V)* stands with the right foot leading and the right hand outstretched as in the Hand Trap game.

The object of the game is for the attacker to bring either the right or the left hand up and strike the victim's outstretched hand before it can be drawn out of the way (see Figure 5).

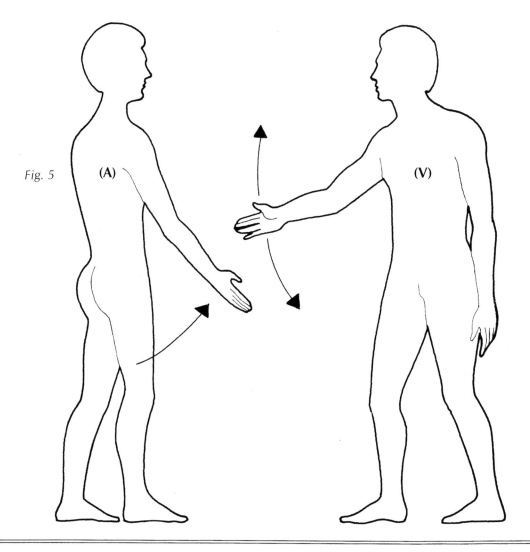

Fig. 5 **(A)** **(V)**

Underhand Tag

This game is commonly seen on school playgrounds and is usually played quite viciously, with the intention of making the backs of the hands good and red with a hefty slap; but for our purposes success is marked by the lightest of touches.

The attacker (A) stands with the right leg leading and extends both arms out with palms turned up. The victim (V) stands facing the attacker with arms outstretched and with the palms turned down and poised over A's palms. The hands do not touch (see Figure 6).

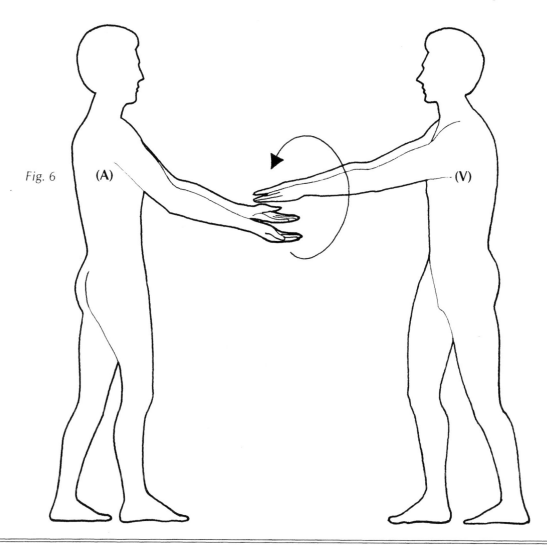

Fig. 6   (A)   (V)

The object of our variation of this game is for the attacker to move the right hand around the victim's left hand and lightly touch the victim's right hand before the victim can move it out of the way. Of course the attacker may also use the left hand to try to touch the victim's right hand.

When first practicing the game, the victim may avoid being touched by moving both hands out of the way at once, but later should move only the hand that is being attacked.

Try to play this game while maintaining eye contact and sensing movements with peripheral vision.

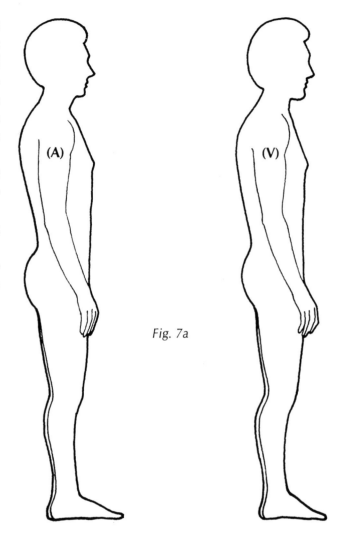

Fig. 7a

Eye Contact Exercise

Eye contact is a stage combatant's first line of defense against accidents. Two combatants should make eye contact before any maneuver to enable them to remain connected and aware of any changes that may occur. This exercise is simply a drill to instill the habit of eye contact among stage fighters. It is wise to practice it before beginning any session of choreography, and especially before practicing slapping, punching, or kicking techniques in combinations.

The attacker *(A)* stands an arm's length behind the victim *(V)* (see Figure 7a). The

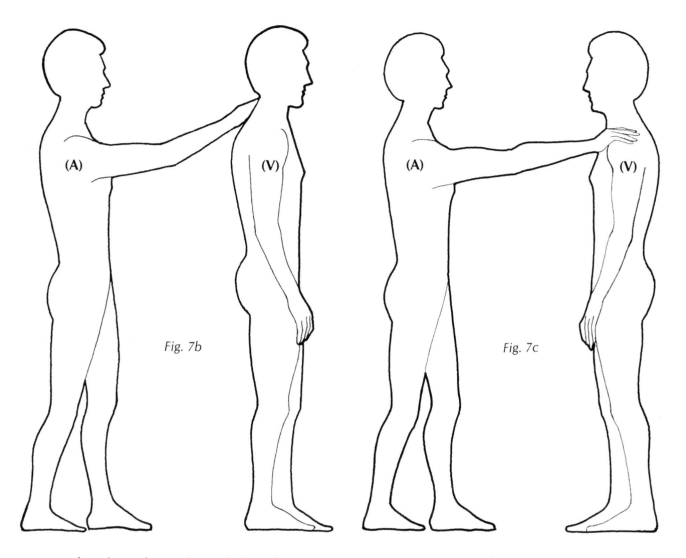

Fig. 7b

Fig. 7c

attacker then places the right hand on the victim's left shoulder, which is a cue for the victim to turn around and face the attacker, pivoting on the right foot (see Figure 7b). When the victim starts to pivot, the attacker drops the right arm and waits for eye contact from the victim. After re- ceiving it, the attacker again grasps the victim's left shoulder with the right hand (see Figure 7c). The victim may wait as long as he or she likes before giving the attacker eye contact.

This game is also a good preparation for practicing the Simple Shoulder Shove.

Techniques and Illusions

Achieve results, but not through violence.
Force is followed by loss of strength.

I THINK THE BEST way to use the illustrations and text that follow is to first read through the description and then picture the actions described in your mind's eye. Next, mimic the foot placement of the attacker and victim in each illusion, and then repeat in slow motion the gestures of the upper body as described, first alone and then with a partner. Pay particular attention to stability, balance, and the safety considerations outlined.

Once a technique is well known and has been practiced in slow motion with a partner many times, exchange roles and try the techniques again in slow motion for a new perspective. Return to your original role, as either the victim *(V)*, or the attacker *(A)*, and practice slowly some more. Both partners may now create the illusion at half speed, so as to synchronize movements and timing.

Now learn several other illusions in the

careful, slow manner described above. Then, after reading the chapter on choreography, put the illusions together to form a combination, so as to discover what adjustments must be made for transitions between techniques.

Be sure to allow enough time. To learn and practice three illusions and combine them with transitions will usually take several hours, especially if you begin (as you should) with a warm-up and a few preparatory partner games.

ROLLING

In practicing rolling and falling, it's best to begin on a soft surface like a tumbling mat or a cushioned carpet over a wooden flooring. If you use carpet, cover your arms and legs to prevent painful carpet abrasions during the early stages of mastering the rolls and falls. Of course, double-check that you have removed all jewelry, belt buckles, keys, pens, pencils, or other hard objects that might be on your person before you begin practice.

Once mastered, the techniques must be practiced on the actual performance surface — usually a wooden stage floor. Never practice or perform on concrete. And don't be ashamed to pad such key areas of the body as knees, shoulder blades, the base of the spine, or the elbows if you feel the need. It's best to accept your limitations early in rehearsal so

that the costume designer has adequate time to work padding into your clothing.

We're attempting to acquire a trusting connection with the ground in rolls and falls. Mastering our natural fear of falling is our first step. So go slowly, and the process will be enjoyable.

The trick of the game is to control and dissipate the impact when the body meets the floor. It should certainly be possible to make a soft landing. A jet liner can do it, and it weighs a great deal more than we do, drops from an unbelievable height with great speed, and lands on concrete. What do we have in common with an airplane? The angle of fall, the ability to roll, and in place of the buoyancy of air pressure on a wing, we have the resistance of our leg muscles.

Standard Forward Roll

Many people, I've discovered, have an innate fear of experiencing the sensations of a complete roll — heels over head. It doesn't pay to push these people despite their fear, but rather it's better to coax them through the steps of a standard forward roll slowly and with the aid of spotters on either side for moral support. A kind and logical approach toward mastering their fears will have an immediate and lasting effect on the performer's response to new techniques.

For a Standard Forward Roll, get down

on one knee with the toes of that foot on the floor. The other leg should be bent with the ball of the foot touching the floor, and both hands should be placed on the floor in front of you, shoulder width apart, much like a sprinter's position in the starting block (see Figure 8a).

Tuck your head well down, chin near chest, and push off with your legs, supporting yourself on your hands, until the momentum of the springing legs causes you to roll over onto your upper back. In this way you avoid touching your head to the floor, but instead pivot on your hands (see Figure 8b). The upper back is the first part of the body to make contact with the mat. The back remains curved, and the weight of the legs circling over the head will cause you to keep rolling until the soles of both feet touch the floor and you stand up (see Figures 8c and 8d).

Many people have no difficulty with a

Standard Forward Roll and can perform it immediately from a kneeling position. Once this is mastered, practice doing the Standing Forward Roll.

Step forward with either your left or right leg (whichever feels more comfortable), bend down, and place both hands on the mat, shoulder width apart. Then tuck your head and roll onto your upper back, down the length of your spine, and onto both feet.

After the Standing Forward Roll is mastered, try it with a short running start, and see how an increase in momentum alters the control of the roll and the recovery to both feet. Usually there is difficulty controlling the forward momentum as you attempt to rise. You can dissipate this momentum by running out of the roll.

When the Running Forward Roll is well under control, go on to the Shoulder Roll.

Shoulder Roll

This is the safest roll for the purposes of combat mime. A Standard Forward Roll is mainly for kinesthetic practice and should always be performed on a soft surface, because it brings the vertebrae of the spinal column into contact with the floor and can therefore cause injury.

The Shoulder Roll, on the other hand, gives added protection to the head, neck, and spinal column. Floor contact proceeds diagonally across the muscles of the shoulder and back, not along the vertebrae.

To prepare for the Shoulder Roll, kneel in the "sprinter's position" as for the Standard Forward Roll, but with one crucial difference: If your right knee is forward as in Figure 9a, lean your head to the left, opening a path to your right shoulder. If the left knee is more comfortable for you, as in Figure 9b, then lean your head to the right. This will also avoid the possibility of accidentally kneeing yourself in the nose.

Fig. 9a

Fig. 9b

Once again use your legs as springs to get your feet over your head, but this time land on the exposed shoulder. Figure 9c is an illustration of a roll on the right shoulder.

After making contact with your right shoulder, roll across your back to your left hip. Tuck your right leg behind your left leg so as to recover from the roll up onto your right knee and left instep (see Figures 9d and 9e).

You'll notice that in the recovery the leg positions are just the opposite of what they were in the preparation position. The left foot is now forward, and you're kneeling on the right knee. The left foot acts as a brake to forward momentum.

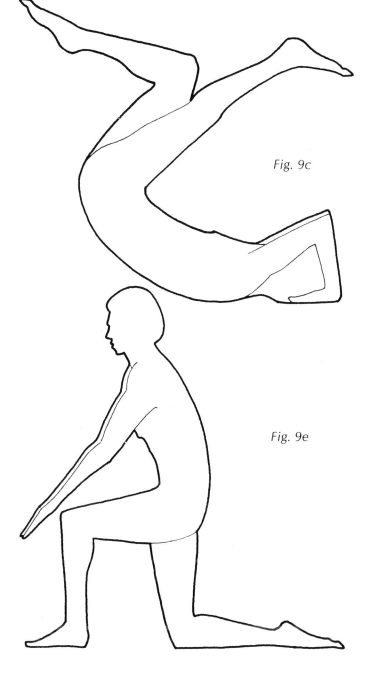

Fig. 9c

Fig. 9e

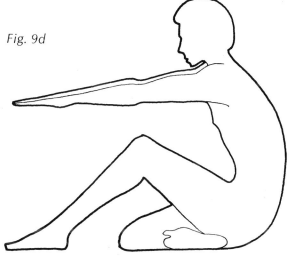

Fig. 9d

A series of Shoulder Rolls can now be practiced down the mat, alternating right and left shoulders. Each recovery will automatically be the preparation position for a roll on the opposite shoulder.

Now try the roll from a standing position. Remember, if you step forward with your right leg to perform the Shoulder Roll, lean your head to the left and control your descent to the ground with your right leg; vice versa for the left shoulder roll. Place both hands firmly in front of you shoulder width apart each time (see Figure 10). Now we're ready for the Dive Shoulder Roll.

Fig. 10

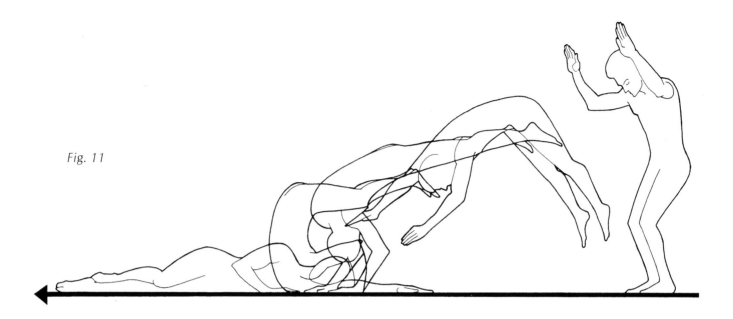

Fig. 11

Dive Shoulder Roll

In order to do a Dive Shoulder Roll, you must spring off both feet from a standing position, travel for a moment completely in the air in a gentle curve toward the ground, then cushion the impact with your arms acting like springs, tuck your head to one side, and roll on the exposed shoulder (see Figure 11).

Try diving over a rolled-up mat, then over a bench, a chair, a suitcase, a barrel, or a horse! Vary the recovery so that you land in a standing position or on one knee.

Fig. 12a

Shoulder Roll without Hands

We did the previous Shoulder Roll from a standing position, making sure to land on both hands, which acted as a pivot and protection for the head. For safety's sake, it is a good idea to use the hands as an aid to the Shoulder Roll, but the hands aren't absolutely necessary. And sometimes it's just not possible to use them because they may be occupied with weapons or props. So it's also a good idea to practice shoulder rolls in which you land directly on the shoulder. The responsibility for controlling the roll now lies predominantly with the leg muscles.

The chin should be tucked closely to the chest, with the head well to the side to expose the shoulder for contact.

By performing a deep plié (knee bend) with the leading leg, you can control the upper body and bring the trunk quite close to the floor (see Figure 12a). Indeed, it's possible to place the exposed shoulder on the floor quite gently, just as you spring forward with the legs to add the necessary momentum for a smooth roll. (see Figures 12b, 12c and 12d).

By only slightly modifying the above Shoulder Roll without Hands, we can do another useful roll, the Aikido Roll.

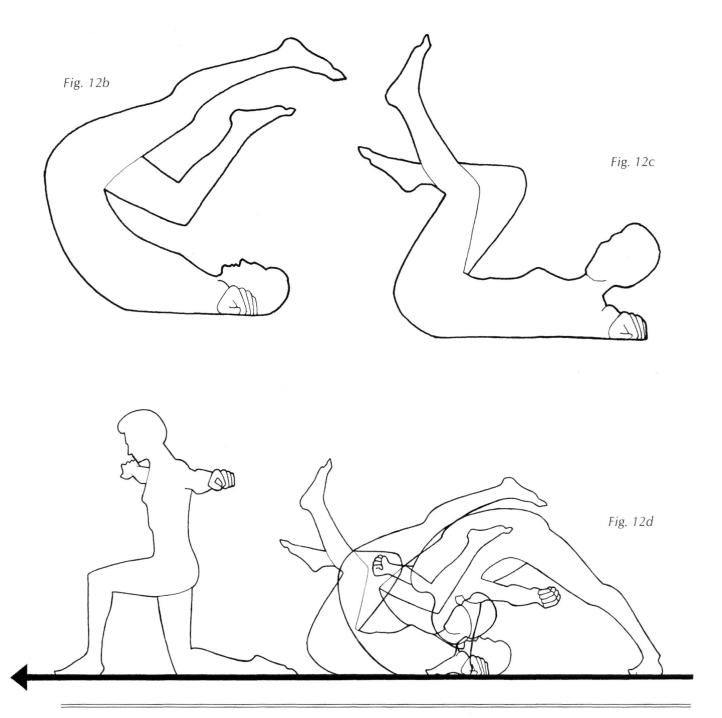

Fig. 12b

Fig. 12c

Fig. 12d

Aikido Roll

When properly executed, this can be an extraordinarily fast roll. It can not only be used as a reaction to a blow or an avoidance of a blow, but it can also be choreographed as a startling offensive move!

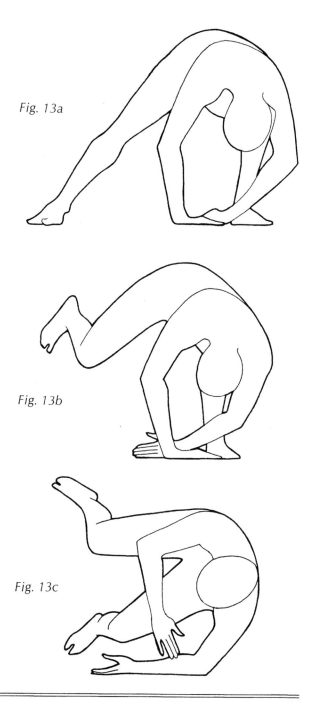

Fig. 13a

Let's begin with a roll on your left side. Place your left foot forward with your left knee bent. Extend your left arm around and under your left knee and reach for the floor with your left hand. It's important to keep your left arm bent all the way through the roll. The right arm remains relaxed and close to the body.

Next, put your head down onto your chest to keep it from striking the mat. One way to keep your head close to your chest is to watch your waist during the roll. After the roll you must look directly ahead to help yourself up (see Figure 13a).

Fig. 13b

Roll by kicking off with your right foot. Roll softly and quietly, with the body in almost a complete circle from the hip to the left arm (Figure 13b).

The roll continues as in Figure 13c.

Regain a standing position by landing on your right knee and putting your left foot forward.

Fig. 13c

FALLING

Once the rolls are mastered, the falls will be easy. However simple it is to master the following falling techniques, they are nevertheless absolutely essential to your safety and should be practiced during every session. Use them as part of your warm-up for each class or rehearsal.

Here's a warning before we begin. There is an instinctual response to falling that we must guard against, namely the panicky desire to thrust out a rigid arm to break a fall. If you give in to this urge, the only thing that may break will be the bones of your arm or wrist. All the following falling techniques are specifically designed so that a rigid arm is unnecessary.

Backward Fall

Our aim is to control this fall all the way to the ground. We don't want to allow the force of gravity even the slightest opportunity to increase our impact with the ground. The opposition to the force of gravity is centered in the resistance of the muscles of the upper thigh, and further control comes from utilizing the principle of counterweight.

Take a healthy step directly backwards with your right foot (all this may be reversed, of course, by stepping back with your left foot), and counterbalance by leaning forward at the waist. Essentially your body weight is pivoting over your right foot (see Figure 14a). Those of you

Fig. 14a

who have taken classes in modern dance will find your practice in contractions very useful here.

Next, sit back gently on your right buttock, counterbalancing by bending your body forward and thrusting your left leg forward (see Figure 14b). This counterbalance will help you control your descent. Sitting back on your buttock protects the base of the spine. Practice the controlled sit several times. There should be no bump when you land. You should have complete control all the way to the floor.

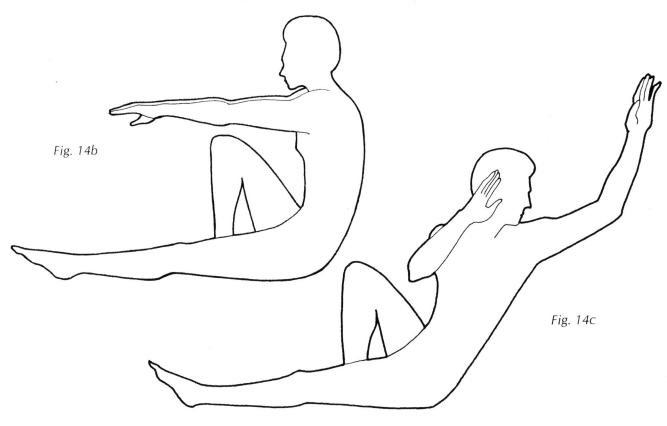

Fig. 14b

Fig. 14c

When the left buttock touches the floor, uncurl sequentially, twist to the left, swing your arms over to the left, and strike the floor with your hands. Finally, stretch out on your left side, with your left arm extended beneath your head to cushion it from any accidental contact with the floor (see Figures 14c, 14d and 14e).

Please notice that the right hand may be used to prevent you from twisting completely over onto your stomach. By ending up on your side, you avoid injuring the spinal column, head, or delicate internal organs. Also please note that the right leg remains bent to further aid you in stabilizing yourself on your side.

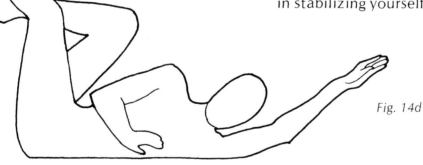

Fig. 14d

Fig. 14e

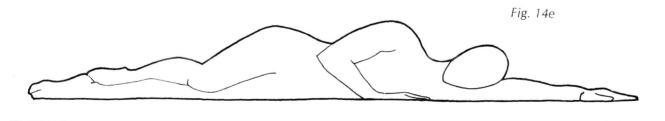

Forward Fall

Take a step forward with your right foot and simultaneously twist your hips to the left, but keep the upper part of your body facing forward, as in Figure 15a.

Then sit on your right buttock just in front of your right heel as in Figure 15b. Note that you are sitting directly down, not launching yourself out into space ahead of yourself.

Finally, reach for the floor in front of yourself and extend your upper body, striking the floor with both hands. Your hands strike the floor as in a Judo Breakfall, creating the sound of impact (see Figure 15c).

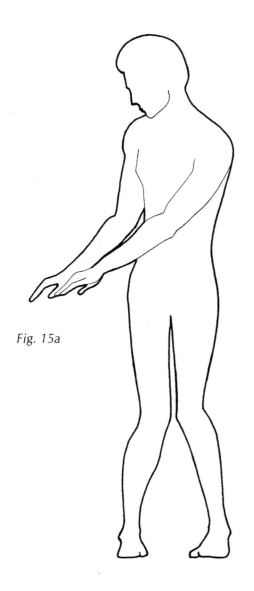

Fig. 15a

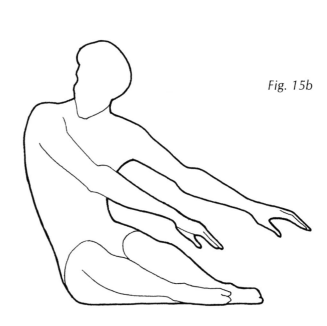

Fig. 15b

Please notice in Figure 15c that you're still somewhat twisted and that neither your elbows nor your knees have struck the ground. (To drop directly onto the kneecaps is very unwise and should be avoided.) And of course keep your head and chin well back to avoid impact with the floor.

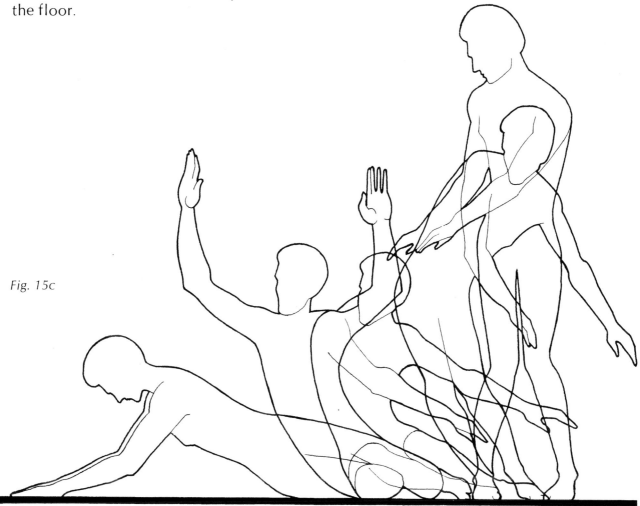

Fig. 15c

Tripping

The old vaudeville stumble combines very nicely with the Forward Fall. To do the stumble, momentarily hook the instep of one foot behind the heel of your other foot, thus breaking the rhythm of your walk to give the illusion of tripping over an obstacle in your path (see Figure 16).

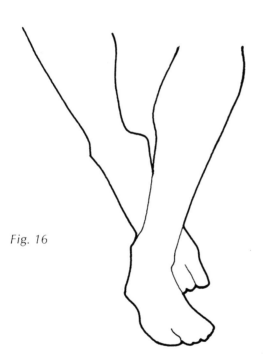

Fig. 16

Side Fall

The Side Fall is taught as a sequential action in modern dance. This technique is ideal for creating the illusion of a dead faint.

If you are going to fall to the right side, shift your weight onto your left foot and bend your left knee to lower yourself to the floor, counterbalancing your weight to the left. Your right upper thigh and buttock should touch the floor lightly (see Figures 17a, 17b and 17c). With practice, you will not have to use your arms for additional support as illustrated.

Continue to lower yourself towards the floor, flowing your weight onto your right arm and sliding out to the right, until you end up resting on your right side, with your right arm beneath your head (see Figures 17d and 17e).

The fainting action should flow smoothly; however, the sitting action shown in Figure 17c happens first, and the slide to the right, as in Figure 17d, follows.

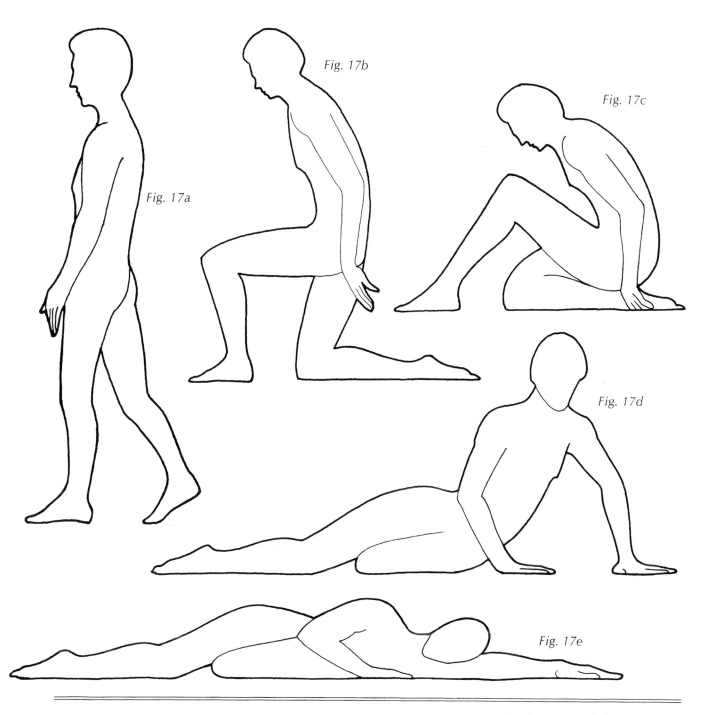

Fig. 17a

Fig. 17b

Fig. 17c

Fig. 17d

Fig. 17e

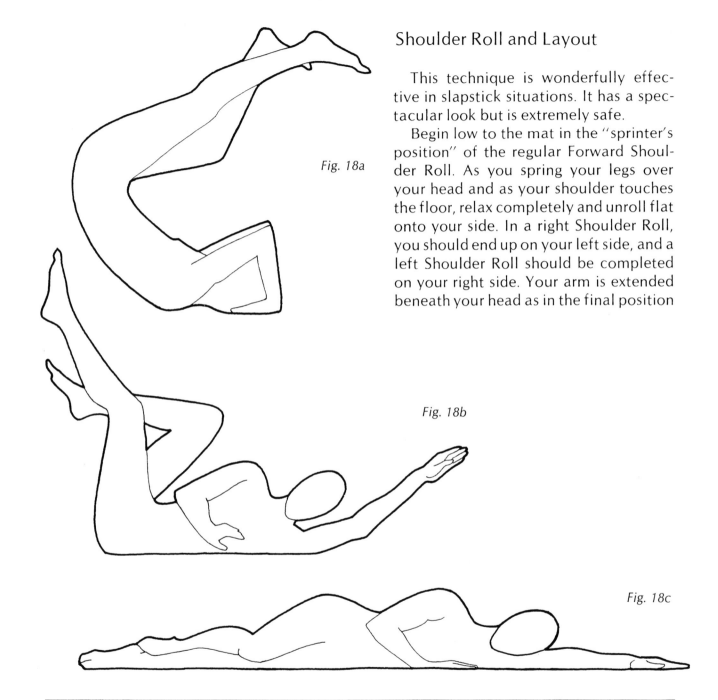

Shoulder Roll and Layout

This technique is wonderfully effective in slapstick situations. It has a spectacular look but is extremely safe.

Begin low to the mat in the "sprinter's position" of the regular Forward Shoulder Roll. As you spring your legs over your head and as your shoulder touches the floor, relax completely and unroll flat onto your side. In a right Shoulder Roll, you should end up on your left side, and a left Shoulder Roll should be completed on your right side. Your arm is extended beneath your head as in the final position

Fig. 18a

Fig. 18b

Fig. 18c

of the Backward Fall (see Figures 18a, 18b, 18c, 18d).

The trick here is to sense when to relax completely so that the body will unroll easily onto the side. It is a natural movement. If you begin the roll on your right shoulder and relax just as your legs pass overhead, the weight of your legs will cause you to roll from the right shoulder onto the left hip.

I might mention that, if you keep the arm extended once it's initially placed on the floor in front of you for the Forward Shoulder Roll, you'll naturally find it will be there for the head to rest on when the layout is completed. The arm should be palm down, to avoid banging the elbow and knuckles. Also, don't become so limp that your legs come crashing down on the heel or outside ankle.

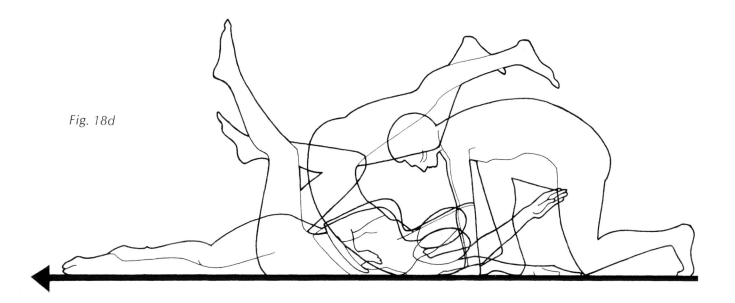

Fig. 18d

BREAKFALLS

The following breakfall techniques can be useful in a great many stage fight situations. They are particularly good to culminate body throws. The loud sounds of impact when the forearms and hands strike the floor never fail to elicit strong reactions from an audience.

A properly executed breakfall will protect a performer from feeling the effect of much of the force of any fall. The important principle to remember is that the arms must strike the ground before the weight of the body. The arms act as springs.

A common error when learning breakfalls occurs when the student instinctively thrusts the hand out to break the force of the fall. This invites injury to the wrist and shoulder. When doing a side or back breakfall the hand and forearm must be in alignment and the impact of the falling body weight is simultaneously taken on the hand and forearm. Also, the hand and forearm are actually striking

Fig. 19a

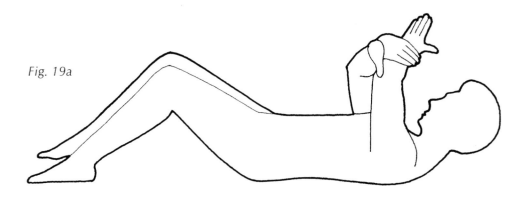

the floor, not merely acting as a rigid prop for the falling body weight. The amount of force with which you strike the floor is determined by the distance of the falling body to the floor.

It's best to begin with a breakfall exercise to become accustomed to striking the floor with the forearms and hands prior to the full body weight contacting the floor.

Lie on your back on a mat or cushioned carpet, with your head up off the mat and your hands crossed in front of your face, palms facing outwards (see Figure 19a).

Now strike the mat fairly gently at first with the fleshy part of the forearms and hands. The forearms and hands must strike the mat at the same time (see Figure 19b).

When practicing try to keep your arms somewhat relaxed. Avoid making the forearms tense and rigid, as this will produce a jarring effect upon the rest of the body. Start with a light striking force, gradually building up the impact.

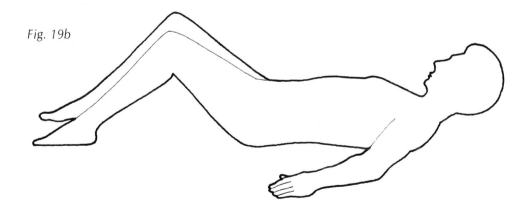

Fig. 19b

Judo Side Breakfall

We will develop this technique in stages. Begin by lying down on your left hip, left arm stretched out palm downwards. Your right hand is in front of your face with the palm facing outwards. Your right leg crosses over your left and the foot is flat to the mat (see Figure 20a).

Now roll over to your right side and strike the mat with your right palm and forearm. When you roll over, your left leg will cross over the right and the left foot will strike the mat at the same time as the right hand and forearm. Your left hand, palm outwards, should cross in front of your face (see Figure 20b).

Practice by rolling from side to side, striking the mat with the left foot and right arm, then the right foot and left arm. Begin slowly and gently, gradually building up speed. Remember to keep your head up off of the mat.

The next stage is to practice the breakfall from a squatting position. Squat down, supporting yourself on the balls of your feet, forearms resting lightly on your knees (see Figure 20c).

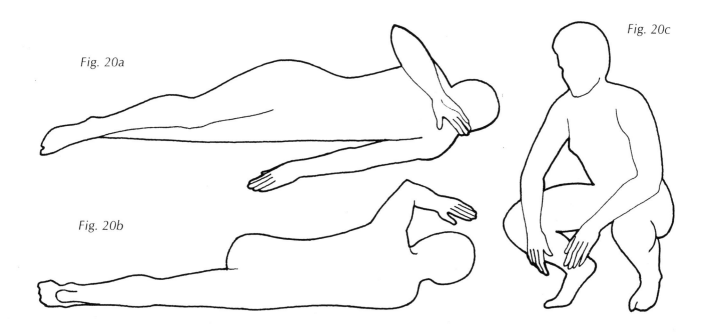

Fig. 20a

Fig. 20b

Fig. 20c

Now shift the weight of your body onto your right foot and bring your left leg forward up off of the mat. As your body begins to fall to the left, bring your left arm up in preparation to strike the mat (see Figure 20d).

Keeping your head well tucked so that it does not hit the mat, strike the mat with your left forearm and hand before the full body weight contacts the mat. Your body shouldn't bounce on the floor, instead roll backwards and to the side allowing your legs to come up. This will minimize any jarring sensations. Now practice this squatting breakfall to the right side.

Once you become comfortable with the squatting side breakfall, begin to practice from a half squat and finally from a standing position (see Figure 20e).

Remember that the farther you fall, the harder the forearm and hand must strike the ground in order to break the fall.

Fig. 20d

Fig. 20e

Judo Front Breakfall

Practice this one on a nice soft surface and work in gradual steps.

Begin in a squatting position, supporting yourself on the balls of your feet, with arms bent, palms downwards, and about shoulder width apart. Now throw yourself forward, striking the mat with the forearms and hands (see Figure 21a).

The hands should strike the mat just in front of the face, before the full body weight makes contact with the mat. Practice the squatting front breakfall until you are absolutely confident with it before moving on to the standing position.

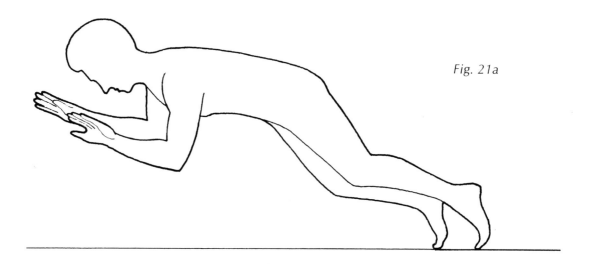

Fig. 21a

From a standing position, leap forward so that you are completely off of the mat (see Figure 21b). You'll absorb the impact of the fall by striking the mat with your palms and forearms about shoulder width apart, and well in front of you on either side of your head. Keep your feet wide apart to help stabilize yourself when you land.

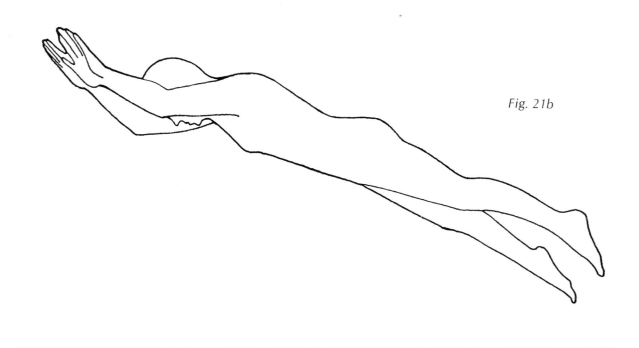

Fig. 21b

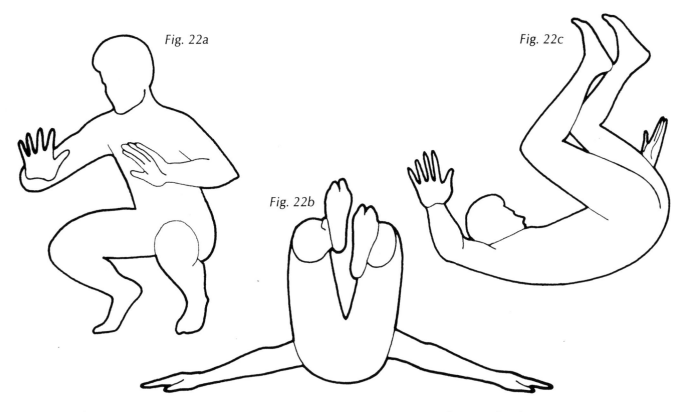

Fig. 22a

Fig. 22b

Fig. 22c

Judo Back Breakfall

This falling technique is particularly useful when creating the illusion of being knocked completely off of your feet backwards. It can also be used to create the illusion of being pushed backwards over someone who is on all fours behind you; a common prank.

Begin by squatting down on the balls of your feet and gently rolling backwards. Break your fall by striking the mat on either side of your body with your hands and forearms (see Figures 22a and 22b).

Keep your chin tucked into your chest to avoid hitting your head on the mat, and continue to roll a bit backwards after your hands and forearms strike the mat.

The next step is to once again start from a squatting position and roll backwards, keeping the seat well tucked so as to avoid landing on the base of the spine (see Figure 22c).

Now try the breakfall from a greater height until you can throw yourself backwards from a full standing position. You should never feel a heavy jarring sensation in your body when you land.

CONTINUAL CONTACT TECHNIQUES

We begin partner training in combat mime with the continual contact techniques because they are the safest of all the procedures when done properly. Also, they are perhaps the simplest to execute with effectiveness, because partners are in physical contact throughout the action, and so it is easy to judge distances. It is also quite simple to detect excessive tension resulting from lack of control. And believe me, you should learn to control tension before you get into the more hazardous punching or kicking techniques.

The continual contact techniques focus on safety right from the start. Therefore, I suggest you begin all your combat rehearsal and training sessions with a few of these techniques until your fights are fully choreographed. They will help you and your combat partner to concentrate and become attuned to each other.

Before we learn the first continual contact illusion, you'll need to be familiar with a few terms:

Eye contact: This is our first and foremost safeguard, and it should precede most combat mime techniques. Eye contact simply means looking into your partner's eyes to acknowledge mutual awareness and readiness to perform the technique. Taking a moment for eye contact not only diminishes the hazard of surprising your partner with an action before he or she is ready, but it also enhances the dramatic rhythms of a fight for an audience.

Eye contact lasts only a moment; then the combatants must look at what they're doing. The attacker must focus on the point of contact in order to be accurate. Don't make the mistake of staring into your partner's eyes while grabbing for the throat, for example.

Develop the habit of establishing eye contact before each and every technique during practice.

Neutral stance: All forms of mime have a particular neutral stance. It should be relaxed and centered, yet energized, and the best base for a particular form of movement. Combat mime has a neutral stance that focuses on stability, balance, and flexibility. It is a comfortable position in which knees are slightly bent and released, feet are shoulder-width apart or a little wider, with one foot in front of the other, and both feet are turned out slightly. The posture is similar to the fourth position in ballet.

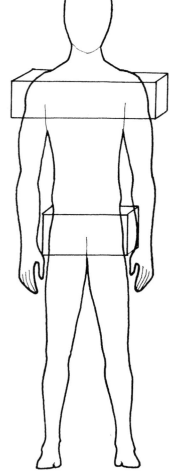
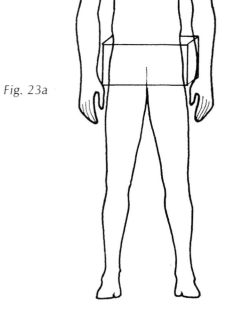

Fig. 23a

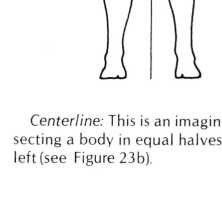

Fig. 23b

Shoulder and hip planes: Seen from the front, the shoulders form an imaginary plane of reference, as do the hips (see Figure 23a).

Centerline: This is an imaginary line bisecting a body in equal halves, right and left (see Figure 23b).

Shoulder Shove

It's helpful to begin partner practice by establishing a mutual trust through basic movements inherent to the continual contact techniques. So please start with a preparatory partner game that uses pushing and pulling between partners in continual contact, such as the Tightrope Wrestle or the Heron Wrestle.

In combat mime, no actual pushing force is ever exerted on the victim. The victim in essence shoves himself or herself, while the attacker merely supports the illusion through mimetic actions. In pulling, choking, or shoving as well, the victim always controls the actions. Often, the attacker's primal instinctual reactions must be superseded by cool reason. The attacker's desire to execute his or her own will upon the victim will be quite strong at times. The attacker quite often "forgets" restraint and begins actually to pull or push the victim to a destination, for example, instead of properly allowing the victim to choose the direction or physical reaction, while the attacker merely supports the illusion as necessary.

For further control, the actions of these combat mime techniques are broken down into movement phrases on a count, just to get you started; in later techniques you'll have to work out the counts yourself.

Simple Shoulder Shove

Here are the four counts of a Simple Shoulder Shove.

1. Establish eye contact. Your may do this from any distance, just as long as both partners register their readiness and connection. Remember to look at the point of contact *before* actually touching the victim (see Figure 24a).

2. The attacker steps to the outside of the victim's right foot and grasps the victim's right shoulder with an outstretched right arm. The force of contact should be agreed upon by both partners, but you can initially grasp

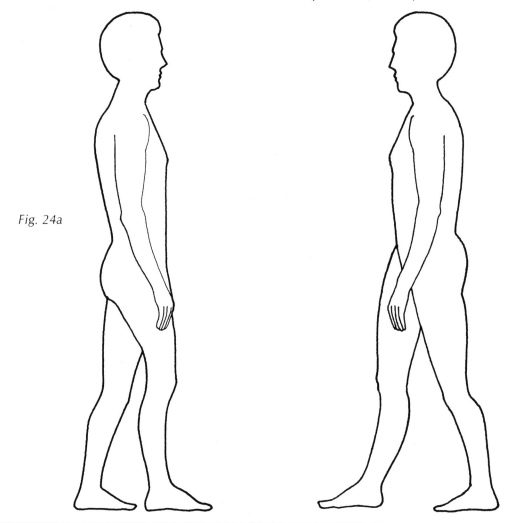

Fig. 24a

your partner's shoulder fairly hard to support the illusion that follows. An initial forceful grasp will enhance the audience's suspension of disbelief, thus "setting the stage" (see Figure 24b).

3. The attacker leans into the victim and bends the elbow, miming the preparation of a shove. The attacker holds the shoulder firmly but doesn't squeeze. The victim mimes resistance by leaning in only slightly. When timed properly, the action looks as though the attacker has grabbed the victim's shoulder and yanked the victim a bit forward in preparation for the shove (see Figure 24c).

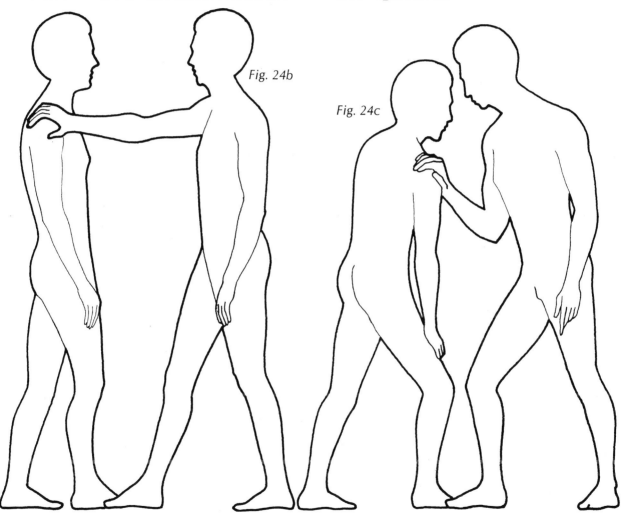

Fig. 24b

Fig. 24c

4. The victim moves backward with the right shoulder leading. Remember that the impetus for the backward movement should appear to come from the right shoulder. The victim completely controls the reaction backward without the aid of the attacker. The attacker follows through with the right arm only after the victim initiates the movement backwards (see Figure 24 d).

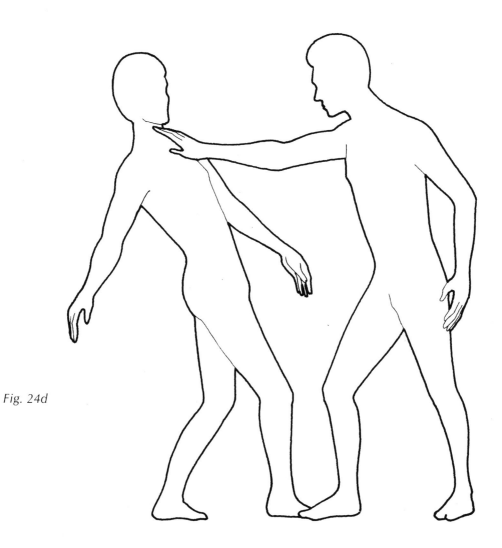

Fig. 24d

Timed correctly, there will be no gap between the actions of the victim and the attacker, and yet no actual resistive force is felt by either partner. After a number of trials and errors, the partners will begin to synchronize the dynamic.

Breaking any such illusion down to a series of counts is an important procedure, regardless of the degree of ferocity or the speed of the technique. However, there is an infinite variety of ways to push someone and any number of areas of the body for initial contact. Please remember five basic points when creating your own variations of the push; some of them are important to remember when creating any stage fight illusion.

1. Work out the foot placement and floor patterns for reactions *before* you try any new move. Of course, all actions are initially rehearsed in *slow motion*.

2. The force of a push travels in a straight line; so the victim must react by leading with the body part opposite the initial point of contact. Also remember that, if both partners use equal dynamics, no force will be necessary or take place accidentally.

3. A common accident, bumping heads, often occurs during the phase of preparation and resistance that ordinarily makes up count two. This can happen when an attacker and victim are parallel and on their centerlines. Always work out reactions before you begin a technique.

4. Always structure a way to protect the victim during the initial contact. Avoid grabbing the victim in sensitive areas such as the throat or face.

5. It is theatrically effective to include just a beat pause during count two (preparation and resistance) to support the illusion. Theatrical timing requires the pause for the audience to appreciate the action as it is happening; otherwise the action may happen too quickly for the audience to follow. In the end, you must trust the eye of the fight director.

Two-Hand Chest Shove

This illusion is commonly used to begin a fight in a bar.

Both the attacker and the victim stand facing each other with their centerlines lined up. The fighting distance is determined by the length of the attacker's arms. The attacker should be able to place both hands upon the victim's chest without stepping forward.

After eye contact, the attacker leans forward and places both hands on the victim's chest, bends both elbows, and leans the head to the left. The victim simultaneously leans slightly forward to mime resistance, and leans the head also to the left, in order to avoid bumping heads with the attacker (see Figure 25a).

Incorrect

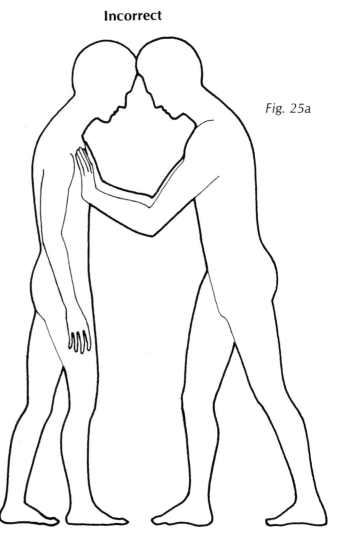

Fig. 25a

Please note that the victim and the attacker both have the right foot forward (see Figure 25b).

The victim then lurches backwards as though being pushed, as the attacker extends the arms forward, straightening the elbows, in a follow-through.

Correct

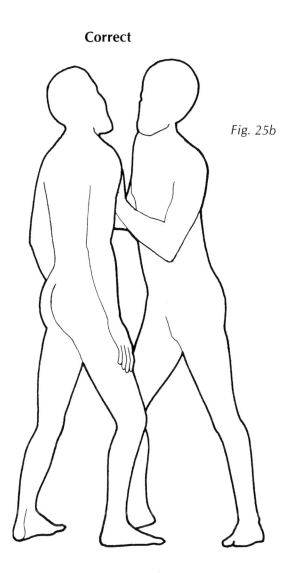

Fig. 25b

Face Shove

The attacker stands facing the victim. Both the attacker and the victim are standing with the right foot leading. After initial eye contact, the attacker reaches forward with the right hand cupped to avoid flattening the victim's nose and places the three middle fingers of the cupped hand on the victim's forehead (see Figure 26). This creates space between the attacker's palm and the victim's nose and eyes.

The victim tilts the head forward slightly as the attacker bends the elbow for count two of preparation and resistance. The victim then jerks the head backwards as if it had been shoved. The attacker simultaneously extends the arm in a follow-through.

Please remember that the victim's body weight must be led backwards by the head, in other words, the head whips backwards first and then the body follows.

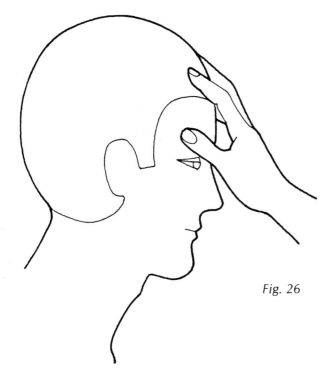

Fig. 26

Foot Shove to Stomach

The attacker stands facing the victim and just to the right of the victim's centerline. Following eye contact, the attacker steps forward onto the left foot and places the right foot in the victim's stomach. The victim simultaneously grabs the attacker's right ankle and bends over as though being kicked in the stomach (see Figure 27).

In this way the victim can control the foot while surreptitiously helping the attacker maintain balance before the reaction.

The victim then jerks backwards, as though shoved in the stomach. The attacker simultaneously extends the right leg in a follow-through only after the victim reacts backwards.

As a further safeguard, the victim should tighten his or her stomach muscles while performing this illusion.

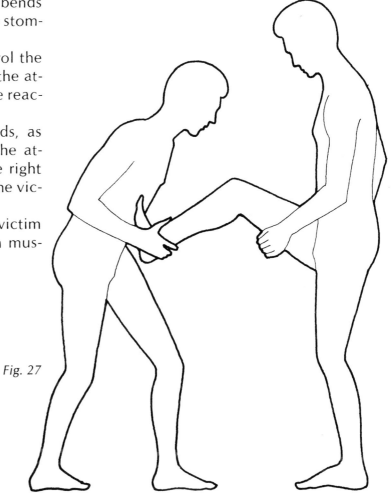

Fig. 27

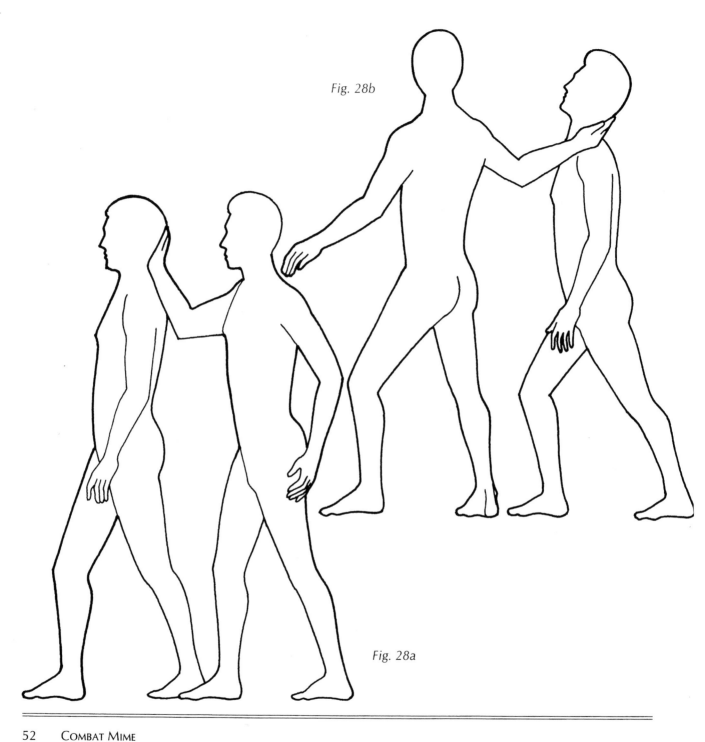

Fig. 28b

Fig. 28a

Head Throw into Shoulder Roll and Layout

This is a combination of the principles of the pushing illusions with techniques of rolling and falling. The action is a classic example of the victim being in complete control as the attacker supports the illusion by miming a follow-through.

The attacker places the right hand at the back of the victim's neck (see Figure 28 a).

The victim runs forward, or in a circle, as though unwillingly propelled by the attacker. The attacker remains slightly in advance of the victim and towards the victim's left side, in this instance, so as not to obstruct the victim's preparation for the shoulder roll (see Figure 28 b).

As the victim, on a prearranged blocking cue, goes into a Shoulder Roll and Layout, the attacker simultaneously slides the right hand up and off the victim's head, without putting even the slightest forward pressure on the victim's head. The attacker then continues to follow through as the victim completes the roll and layout (see Figure 28 c).

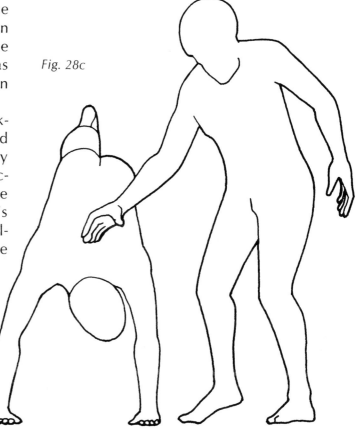

Fig. 28c

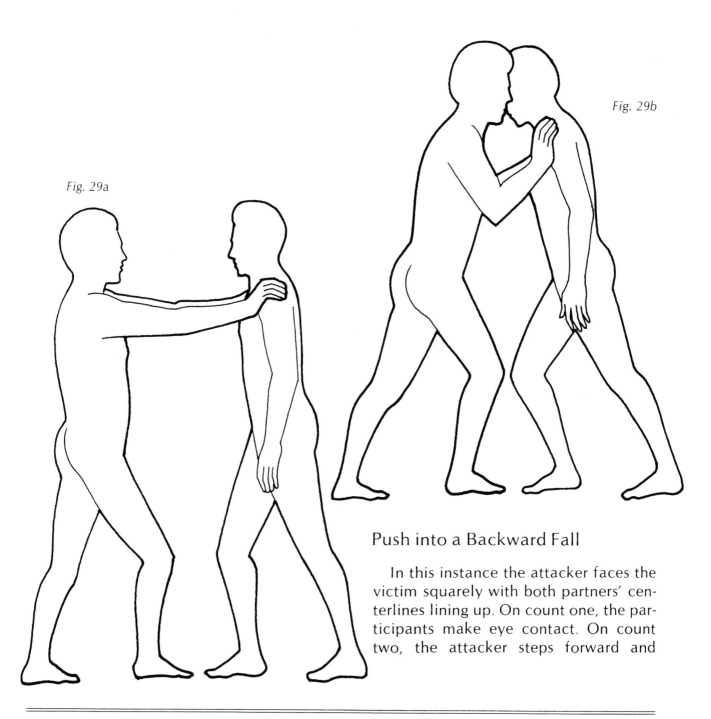

Fig. 29b

Push into a Backward Fall

In this instance the attacker faces the victim squarely with both partners' centerlines lining up. On count one, the participants make eye contact. On count two, the attacker steps forward and

Fig. 29c

places both hands on the victim's shoulders or upper chest (see Figure 29 a). On count three, the attacker bends both elbows without putting any pressure on the victim (see Figure 29 b). Remember to decide beforehand to which side you'll both angle your heads to avoid bumping.

On count four the victim steps back and performs a backward fall as the attacker extends both arms in the follow-through and bends forward at the waist and at the knee of the leading leg (see Figure 29 c).

Push over a Bench
to a Side Breakfall

If a victim is being pushed over a low stool, bench, etc., the distance between the victim and the object must be carefully worked out beforehand, so that the victim can know how many backward steps are needed to reach the object without having to look. Let's practice with a low, stable bench.

After walking backwards to the bench, the victim sits down on it, twists the upper part of the body, and looks where he or she is going to land (see Figure 30 a). Then the victim reaches for the floor as in a Judo Side Breakfall and strikes the floor with the hand and forearm, dissipating the force of impact (see Figure 30 b). It is a good idea for the victim to continue to dissipate the force of the fall and avoid knocking over the bench, by rolling along the floor.

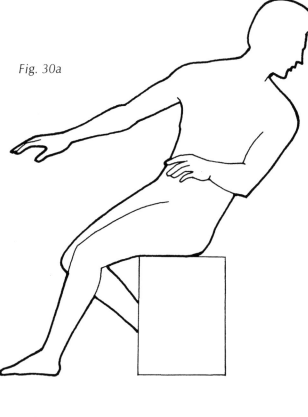

Fig. 30a

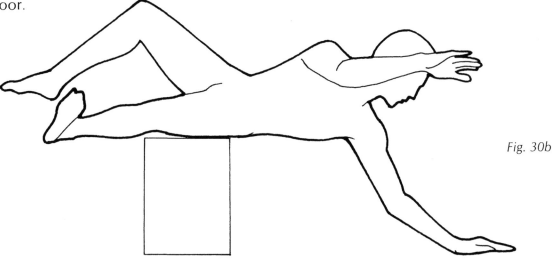

Fig. 30b

Push from Behind
into a Forward Fall

Since eye contact preceding this technique is impractical, it is sometimes helpful to add a physical cue in lieu of it. The signal should be a touch on some part of the victim's body not involved in execution of the technique; e.g., the attacker can, with the leading foot, touch the victim's heel. The next step is to place one or both hands on the victim's back for count two (see Figure 31 a).

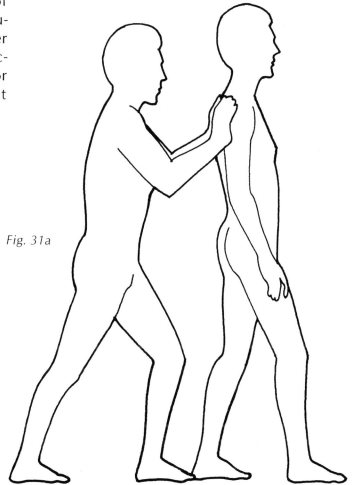

Fig. 31a

The attacker on count three bends the elbows and leans into the victim, as the victim leans back slightly (see Figure 31 b). Remember, there should be no weight transfer between victim and attacker. The victim then performs a Forward Fall as the attacker extends both arms in a follow-though (see Figure 31 c).

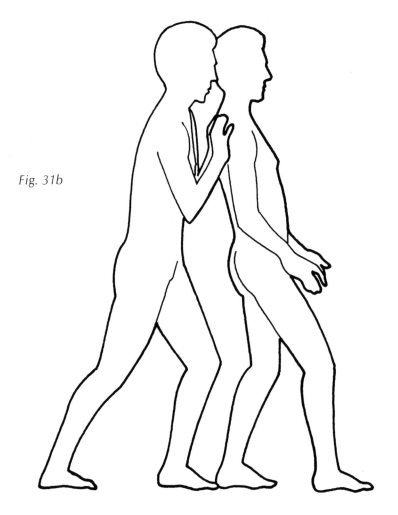

Fig. 31b

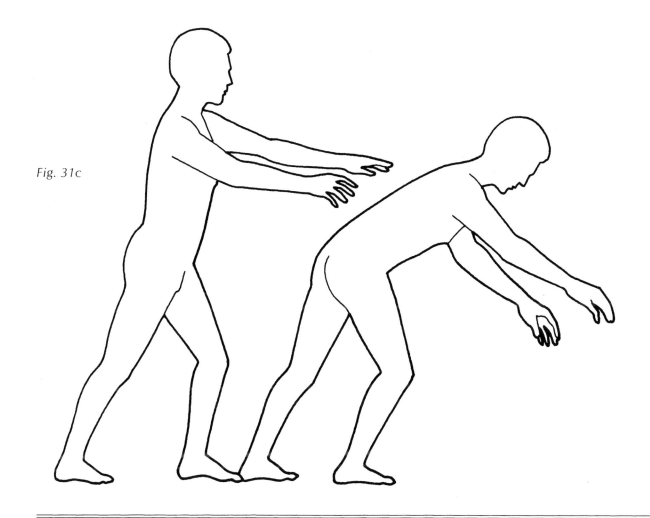

Fig. 31c

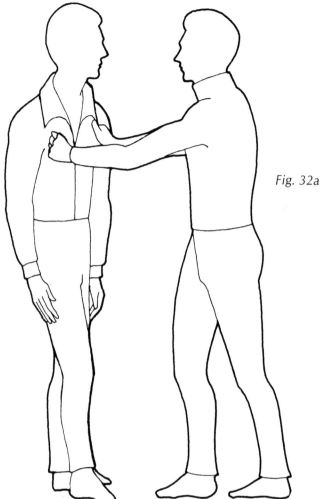

Fig. 32a

Pulling Clothing

This technique may be used in a variety of ways and situations. It is sometimes used as a transitional technique for an overhead foot throw. It also can be used as a preparation for pushing a villain up against a wall.

The attacker and victim stand opposite one another and establish eye contact. Then the attacker steps forward and grabs the victim's shirt with both hands (see Figure 32 a). The attacker twists the material, which creates the illusion that the clothing is being pulled (see Figure 32 b). The attacker then relaxes the arms but keeps the fists against the victim's chest. The victim may grab the attacker's wrists to help the attacker maintain contact with the chest (see Figure 32 c). A pulling, pushing, or throwing technique may now be executed.

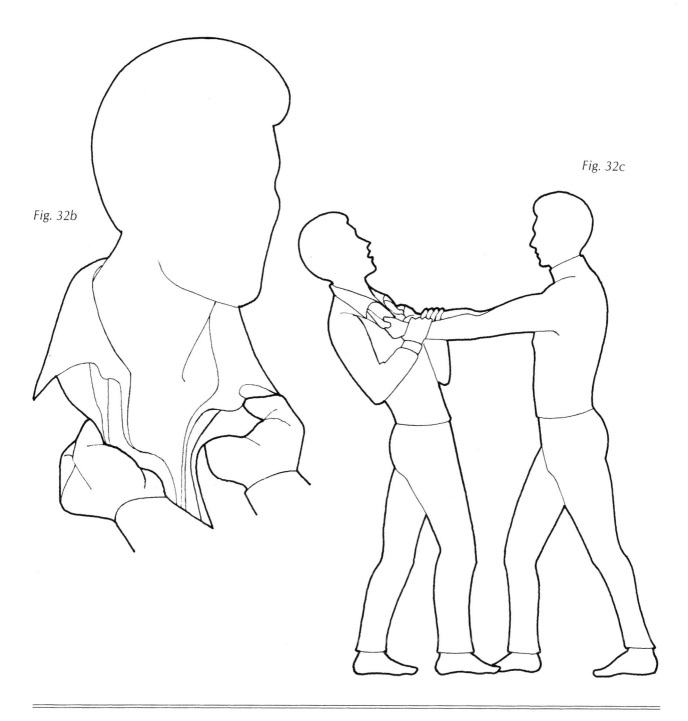

Fig. 32b

Fig. 32c

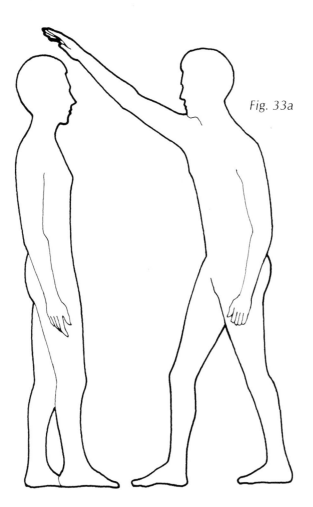

Fig. 33a

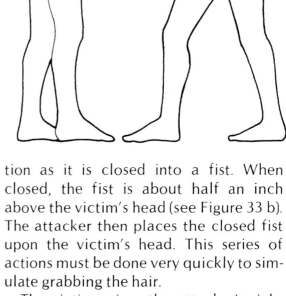

Fig. 33b

Pulling Hair

This technique is an entirely painless illusion that relies heavily on the performers' acting abilities. It lends itself to a thousand styles and situations.

The attacker reaches above the victim's head with the right hand, fingers wide apart, palm down (see Figure 33 a). The hand describes a rapid circular motion as it is closed into a fist. When closed, the fist is about half an inch above the victim's head (see Figure 33 b). The attacker then places the closed fist upon the victim's head. This series of actions must be done very quickly to simulate grabbing the hair.

The victim seizes the attacker's right wrist with the left hand, so as to keep the action visually open to the audience. The illusion created is that the victim is trying

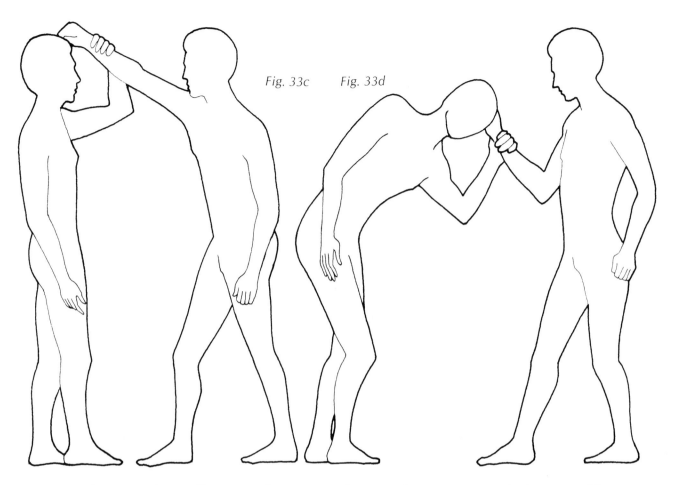

Fig. 33c Fig. 33d

to ease the pain by pulling on the attacker's arm or working to loosen it. Actually, the victim is holding the attacker's fist to the head with a comfortable pressure (see Figure 33 c). It is the victim's responsibility to keep the attacker's fist in contact with the head during the ensuing gyrations, so as not to destroy the illusion.

The victim now moves *toward* the attacker, with the head leading the body, as the attacker retreats, miming a pulling action but with a completely relaxed arm (see Figure 33 d).

Remember, we rely heavily on vocal and physical pain reactions from the victim, as well as accurately mimed physical aggression from the attacker, to carry off this illusion. And look where you're going! Don't be so absorbed by the hair pulling and acting that you bump into objects or other actors or fall off the stage.

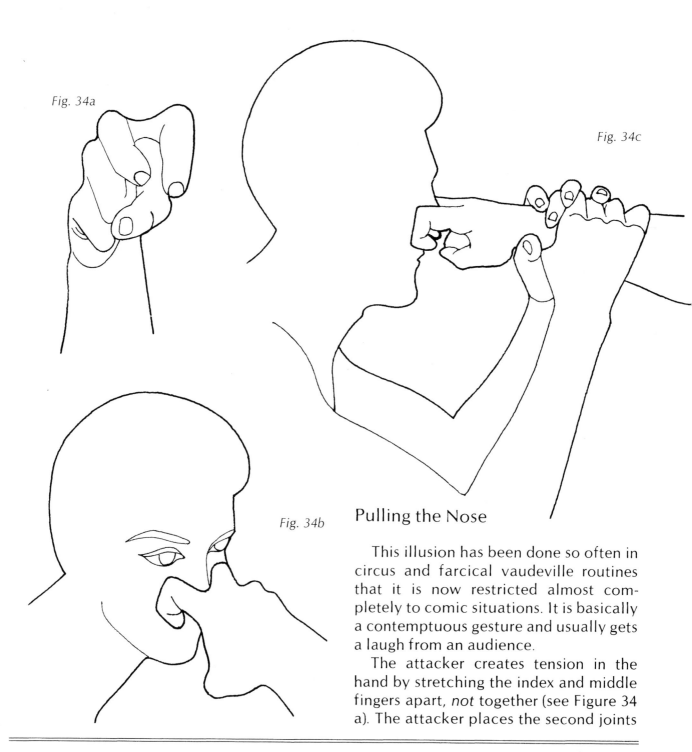

Fig. 34a

Fig. 34c

Fig. 34b

Pulling the Nose

This illusion has been done so often in circus and farcical vaudeville routines that it is now restricted almost completely to comic situations. It is basically a contemptuous gesture and usually gets a laugh from an audience.

The attacker creates tension in the hand by stretching the index and middle fingers apart, *not* together (see Figure 34 a). The attacker places the second joints

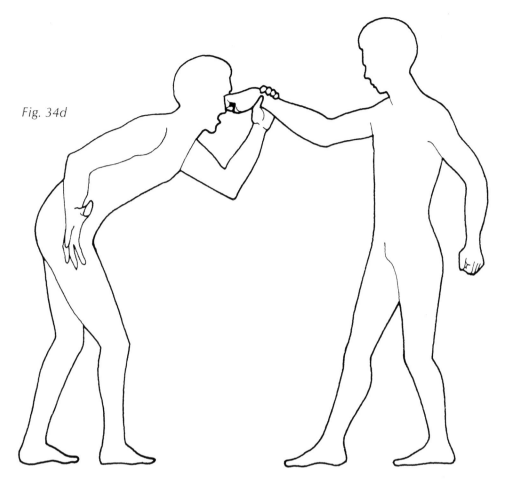

Fig. 34d

of the index and middle fingers on either side of the bony ridge of the victim's nose, being careful not to push against the victim's face (see Figure 34b).

The victim grabs the attacker's wrist and presses the rigid hand against the face with a comfortable force (see Figure 34c). It is the responsibility of the victim to protect his or her own eyes and face by correct tension and positioning of the attacker's hand.

The attacker then relaxes the arm com-

pletely and allows the victim to mime pain and direct the movement. The victim should move toward the attacker to simulate the pulling action, and the attacker retreats, miming the strain (see Figure 34d).

A vocal expression of pain is extremely important to the drama and believability of this technique. The sound should be somewhat nasal, as the nose is supposedly being pinched.

Pulling an Ear

The attacker stands directly facing the victim and reaches with the right hand toward the victim's left ear. The attacker then creates a hollow cup with the fingers and thumb of the right hand (Figure 35 a) and places the cup over the victim's ear. In essence, the attacker is protecting the victim's ear from harm (see Figure 35 b).

The victim then grasps the attacker's right wrist with the left hand, so as to remain visually open to the audience, and holds the attacker's cupped hand over the ear with a comfortable pressure (see Figure 35 c). The victim must make sure not to break the contact and spoil the illusion.

The victim then winces, screams, shouts, etc., and moves toward the attacker, leading with the ear (as though being pulled by the ear). The attacker relaxes the right arm, without removing the hand from the ear, and follows the victim's impetus by miming a pulling action (see Figure 35 d). Whatever happens, the attacker must not squeeze the ear or push or pull the victim.

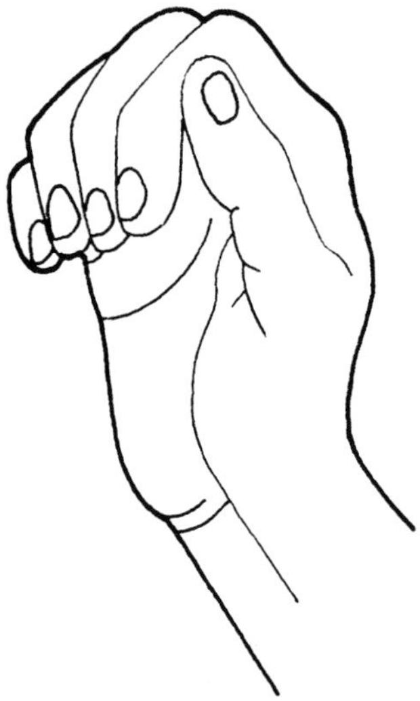

Fig. 35a

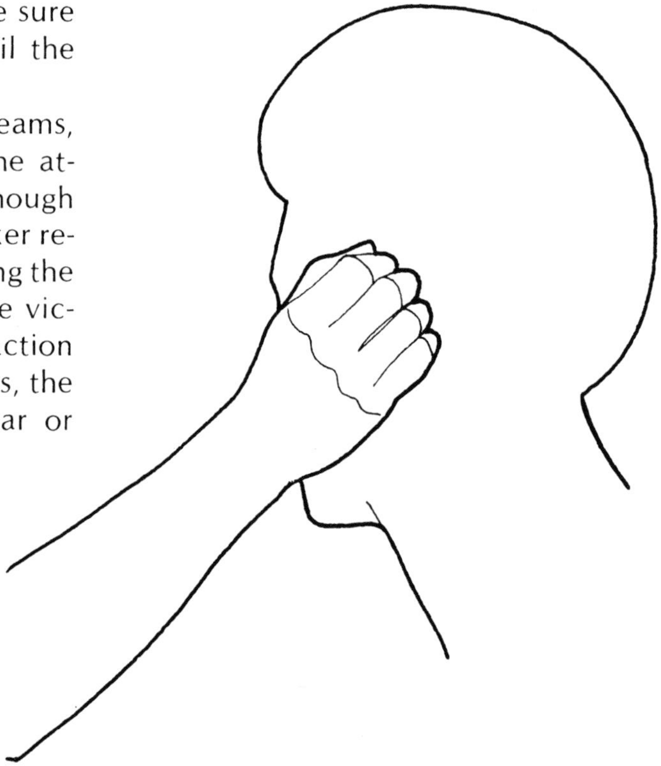

Fig. 35b

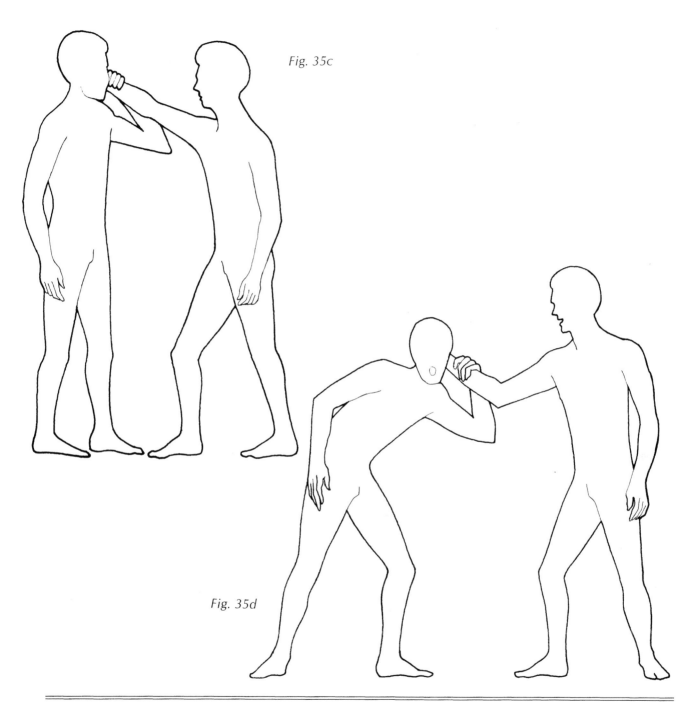

Fig. 35c

Fig. 35d

Restraining Wrestle, Traveling

Attempting to force someone across the stage in a quasi-standing wrestle is a very common occurrence in drama. Unfortunately, it's also common to see two actors trip over their own feet while trying to accomplish this and go tumbling painfully to the floor. One can avoid this mishap by working out the floor patterns of the victim's and the attacker's feet and by practicing a twist in the lower body.

In Figure 36 a, the attacker is clutching the victim in a bear hug and both are trying to use the same floor space to walk in; tripping is almost inevitable. I do not suggest you do it this way, as a bloody nose from heads banging together is also pretty likely.

Instead, as in Figure 36 b, the attacker stands to one side of the victim; twisting the upper half of the body toward the victim, to create the bear hug illusion. Yet from the hips down the attacker's body is pointed in the direction both combatants will be traveling. Both attacker and victim may now walk in their own paths without stumbling over each other's feet. Also note that the attacker angles the head slightly away from the victim to allow the victim to mime the gyrations of struggling without fear of being bopped in the nose.

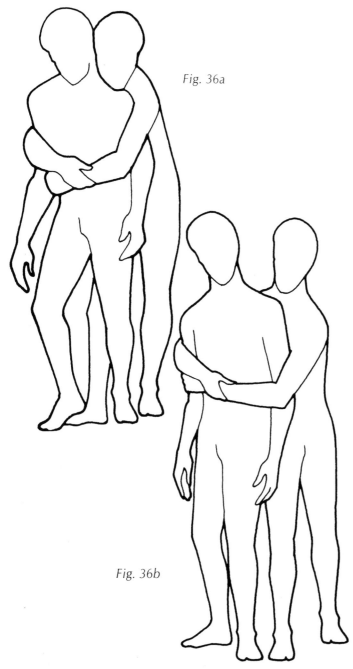

Fig. 36a

Fig. 36b

Bending an Arm behind the Back

The disciplines of judo, hapkido, and jujitsu have many ways of leading into this action, and exploring any of the above martial arts would immeasurably aid the student of stage combat. Nevertheless, keep in mind at all times that in combat mime the victim initiates the "pain-inflicting action" while the attacker relaxes and follows the victim. This is all one needs to improvise any lead-in.

The attacker stands facing the victim, steps forward with the right foot, and grabs the victim's left wrist (see Figure 37 a).

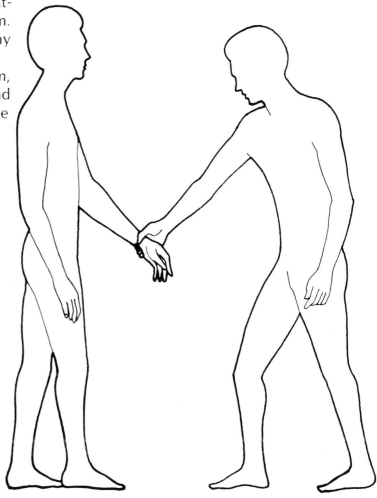

Fig. 37a

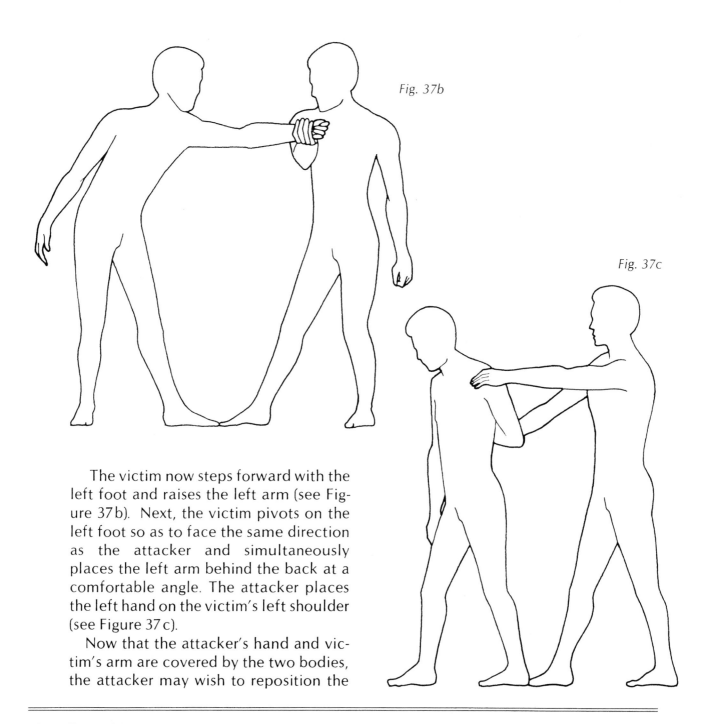

Fig. 37b

Fig. 37c

The victim now steps forward with the left foot and raises the left arm (see Figure 37b). Next, the victim pivots on the left foot so as to face the same direction as the attacker and simultaneously places the left arm behind the back at a comfortable angle. The attacker places the left hand on the victim's left shoulder (see Figure 37c).

Now that the attacker's hand and victim's arm are covered by the two bodies, the attacker may wish to reposition the

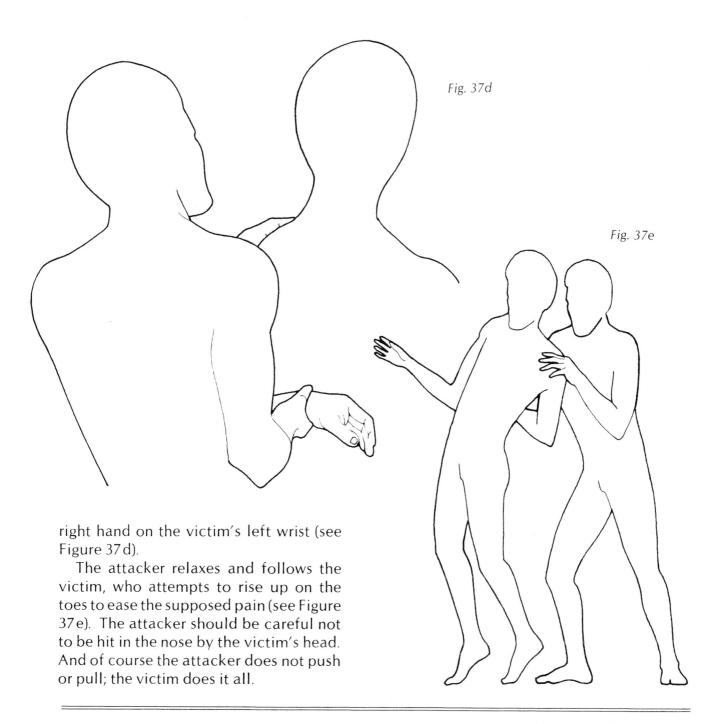

Fig. 37d

Fig. 37e

right hand on the victim's left wrist (see Figure 37d).

The attacker relaxes and follows the victim, who attempts to rise up on the toes to ease the supposed pain (see Figure 37e). The attacker should be careful not to be hit in the nose by the victim's head. And of course the attacker does not push or pull; the victim does it all.

Biting

This is a commonsense technique that is ridiculously simple to perform but never fails to get a great audience reaction as long as the acting is convincing. Any fleshy area of the victim's body can be used to simulate a bite, but we will take a look at biting the forearm.

The attacker holds the victim's forearm and places the open mouth, lips pulled back to expose the teeth, over the flesh of the forearm (see Figure 38 a). The actors then mime the action.

You can increase audience suspense by placing the victim's free hand on the attacker's forehead and miming the action of attempting to push the attacker's head back away from the arm (see Figure 38 b). The attacker must not allow the tensions engendered in any struggle to cause the jaws to close. However, the attacker, not the victim, controls the victim's forearm. In this case, the victim must relax the forearm and allow the attacker to lead. The victim does not push at all on the attacker's head. The attacker moves his own head back as the victim mimes a pushing action with a relaxed arm.

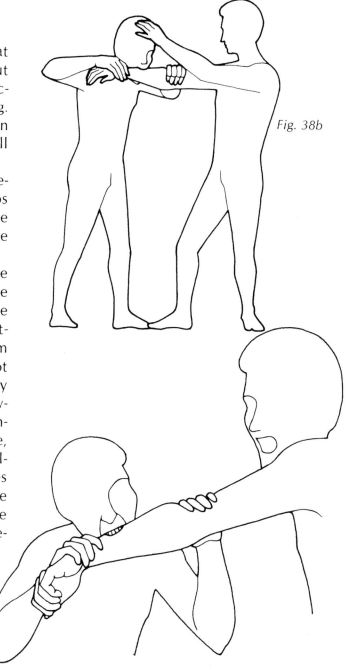

Fig. 38b

Fig. 38a

Choking, Both Hands from the Front

The front portion of the neck is a vulnerable area. The trachea and vocal chords are somewhat exposed, and there are many delicate glands just beneath the surface in the throat area; therefore the front portion of the neck is never held or struck. Instead we concentrate on those heavier muscles of the upper shoulders and the lower portion of the back of the neck, the trapezius muscles. The collarbone may also be used as a point of contact for support.

Initially, the attacker faces the victim – although once the technique is fully learned the attacker may choke a victim from the back, or from any position. Next, the attacker steps forward with the right foot and places both hands around the victim's lower neck, resting outside edges of the hands on the collarbone with a firm pressure (see Figure 39 a).

The fingers grasp the muscles of the upper shoulders on either side of the victim's neck as the attacker's hands form a rigid circle, protecting the trachea. The thumbs are crossed in front of the neck, and the inner thumb forces out isometrically against the outer, overlapping thumb. The outer thumb is not pushing in towards the throat (see Figure 39 b). Thus the attacker's energy is not actually con-

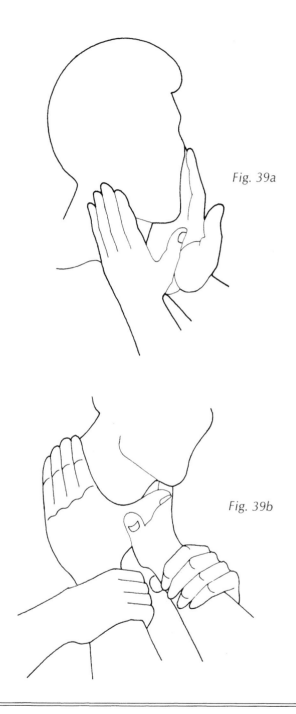

Fig. 39a

Fig. 39b

centrated on closing the hands around the neck, as it appears, but in pushing downward.

The victim then lowers the chin to hide the gap between the attacker's thumbs and the throat, without actually closing it (see Figure 39c). The choking is now mimed as the victim grasps the attacker's wrists and presses the attacker's hands down onto the victim's upper chest (not into the throat) with a comfortable force, so as to maintain contact throughout any ensuing struggle (see Figure 39d).

The attacker never squeezes the hands together. The victim must not allow the front of the neck to touch the attacker's hands. The attacker must relax the arms to allow the victim complete freedom of movement. The attacker can effectively mime the choking action with the shoulders heaving, timed, of course, to coincide with the victim's choked vocalizations and physical reactions.

Be careful not to let the victim's head flop around much, as the head is a heavy object and can all too easily strain the neck muscles.

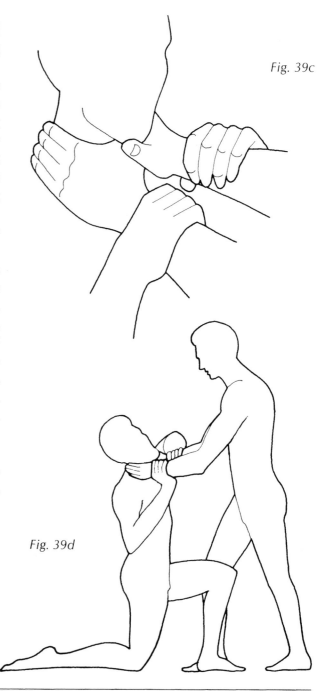

Fig. 39c

Fig. 39d

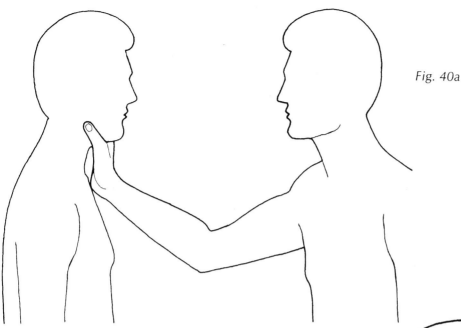

Fig. 40a

Choking, One Hand from the Front

Only a fairly robust attacker appears credible in this technique because choking with only one hand would require a great deal of strength if performed in actuality.

The attacker stands opposite the victim in a neutral stance and establishes eye contact. The attacker then bends the wrist to a ninety-degree angle or as close to it as possible, forming a cup shape with the hand, and places the outside edge of the palm on the collarbone. The thumb and fingers rest on the muscles of the neck to either side of the trachea (see Figures 40 a and 40 b). Notice the gap between the palm of the attacker's hand and the victim's throat.

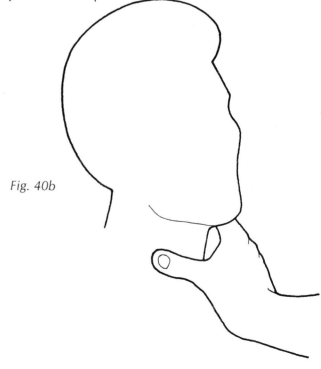

Fig. 40b

The victim then grabs the attacker's wrist with both hands and holds the edge of the attacker's palm down on the collarbone. The attacker relaxes the arm from the shoulder and elbow, while the victim lowers the chin to hide the gap between the attacker's palm and the victim's throat (see Figures 40c and 40d).

Of course the victim then controls the direction of any struggling movements, while the attacker merely relaxes and mimes tension and effort, taking cues from the victim

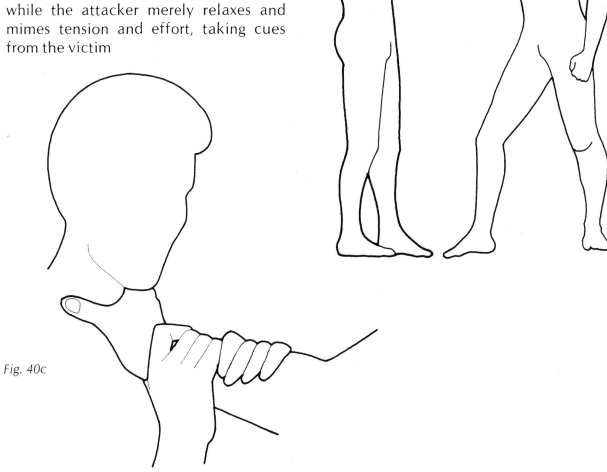

Fig. 40d

Fig. 40c

Forearm Choke from Behind

A variation on choking with the hands is choking with the forearm. Again we follow the principle of applying pressure to a portion of the anatomy more solid than the neck. Plan to use a physical cue in lieu of eye contact.

In this case, the attacker's left arm is across the victim's upper chest along the collarbone, below the neck (see Figure 41 a). The attacker's left hand grasps the victim's right shoulder. The victim grasps the attacker's arm and holds it firmly upon the victim's upper chest (see Figure 41 b). The attacker channels pressure into squeezing the victim's right shoulder and thereby anchoring the arm in a position that will protect the neck during any choreographed struggle.

The victim "covers" the neck by lowering the chin onto the attacker's forearm (see Figure 41 c).

Discover for yourself other ways of protecting the neck in choking positions.

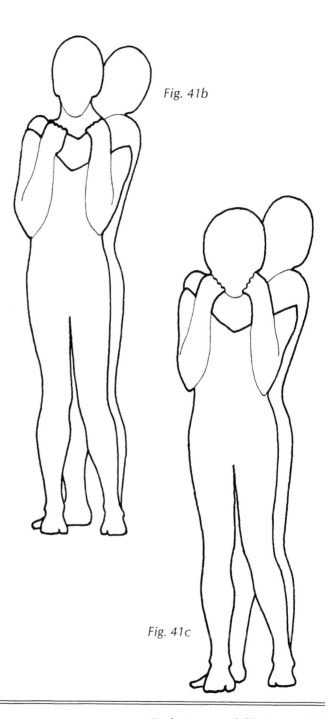

Fig. 41b

Fig. 41c

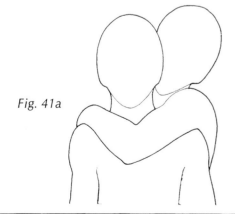

Fig. 41a

Shove Up against a Wall

This illusion is often used on television as a prelude to an interrogation on the street between tough cops and some petty criminal. You'll find it adds spice to many confrontations and is very effective as a transitional move during a longer fight.

Let's use, as a setup, the technique of Pulling Clothing, although Choking, Both Hands from the Front or various other techniques could also be used.

Both attacker and especially victim have paced off the distance to the wall. As the victim approaches the wall, the buttock muscles are tensed in order to protect the lower spine and the shoulders

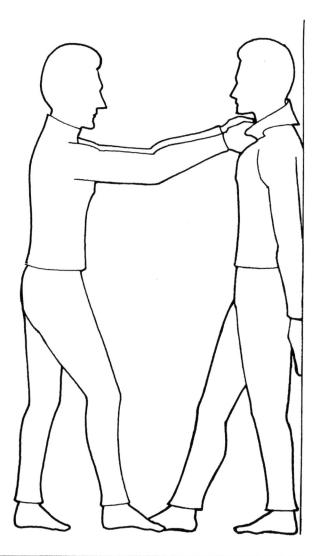

Fig. 42a

are pulled back to tighten the trapezius muscles, thereby flattening the shoulder blades so that their tips won't bang into the wall. The victim also keeps the head slightly forward so it will not strike the wall. And need I add that the victim, not the attacker, is controlling the action?

At the same time that the buttocks and back muscles hit the wall, the victim strikes it with flat palms to dissipate the impact (see Figure 42 a). The attacker then bends both knees, sinking down, and straightens both arms at the elbow. Simultaneously the victim rises on the toes. Together they create the illusion that the attacker has lifted the victim up against the wall (see Figure 42 b).

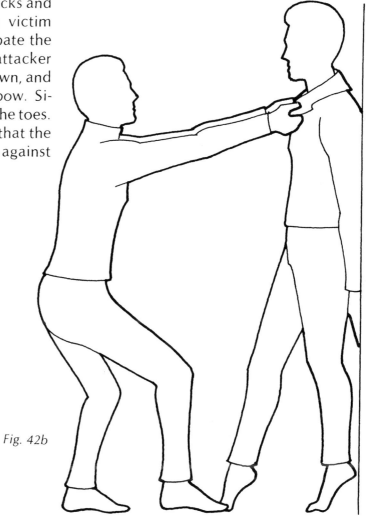

Fig. 42b

SCRATCHING AND SLAPPING

A great many theatrical domestic quarrels are resolved through violence in the form of scratching or slapping. Even if a performer is never called upon to do a full stage fight, most will very likely be asked to begin or end a quarrel with one of the following techniques.

In difficulty these illusions belong between continual contact and punching. Less force is involved in scratching and slapping than in punching, but the element of fighting distance becomes an important safety factor for the first time.

Fighting distance is the space between the combatants, which must be judged accurately to safely create the illusion of contact. It is important to become proficient at judging fighting distance, since the margin for error is sometimes less than an inch. Never assume that you can judge it without practicing in slow motion first. It doesn't require much of an error to clip your partner on the tip of the nose with a sharp fingernail. In fact, it is especially important that fingernails be short and smooth during these exercises.

Go back and practice the preparatory partner game Shoulder Tag to tune in to speed, control, and accuracy within a prescribed fighting distance.

Scratching

In conjunction with a severe pain reaction like a horrified scream or an agonized cry, or with a blood effect, this can be a truly effective and shocking illusion.

The scratching action may be done without making any contact, which is the safest method, especially around the eyes. Or the attacker may lightly and quickly stroke the victim's face, neck, chest, etc. (not the eyes) with the pads of the fingertips. In either case, the attacker should "scratch" while the wrist is bent. Instead of curling the fingers and moving the hand and arm together across the victim's body, the attacker should bend the wrist and slightly spread the fingers of the striking hand, presenting the fingerpads to the victim. This maneuver is what creates the illusion of scratching. Whether the attacker is making contact or not, the bent wrist thwarts the audience's depth perception.

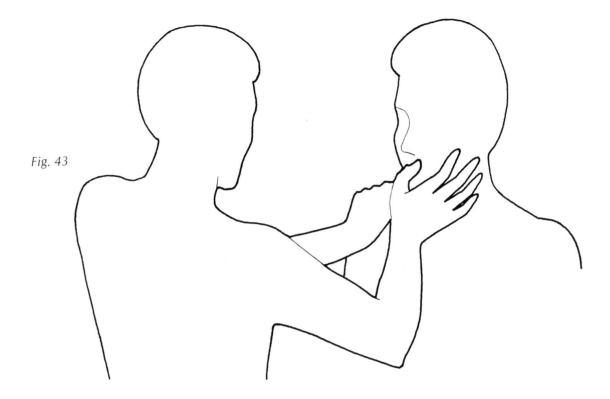

Fig. 43

If the face is being "scratched," the attacker's hand should be drawn straight back toward the attacker's own left shoulder to minimize the risk of injuring the victim. To solidify fighting distance, I suggest that the attacker maintain continual contact by holding the victim's right arm or shoulder, as shown in Figure 43.

Timing is essential to the believability of the scratching illusion. There should be a beat pause when the attacker's hand reaches the victim's face. The victim should then jerk the head to the side, at the same time as the attacker draws the hand back, creating the illusion of fingernails raking through the flesh of the cheek.

Slapping

In my experience, the slap is the most common and the most abused combat mime illusion. My pet peeve as a stage fight choreographer is the director who insists that a slap be executed in reality every night of performance and yet waits until dress rehearsal to have the performers execute it because the pain involved frightens them. More often than not, he gives no instructions about the amount of force to be used or the area of the face to be hit — as though a slap were an intuitive function inherently known from birth!

I will admit there are times when performing an actual contact slap may be essential. During rehearsal, the resulting shock, pain, indignation, and shame may be crucial to the actor's or actress's internal character development. In an extremely intimate theater space a contact slap may be the only believable action. However, with enough rehearsal the noncontact slapping illusion can be effective even on an arena stage.

Nevertheless, the slapping action itself is very critical, and although I personally do not advocate an actual slap during a performance, I will discuss this option before describing the noncontact alternatives.

Contact Slap

Fight choreographers who advocate using contact with slapping disagree about what area of the body to strike. I suggest that only two areas of the human head and neck are comparatively safe to strike — the cheek and jaw, and the back of the neck to either side of the spinal column.

In slapping the cheek, the fingertips may not extend beyond the cheekbone, nor should the little finger of the striking hand touch below the jawline (see Figure

44 a). It should be obvious that we are trying to protect the eyes, eardrums, nose, and mouth. The impact occurs with fingers firmly together and the thumb off to one side, not curled in front of the palm (see Figure 44 b).

Fighting distance is crucial because it affects accurate placement of the hand on contact. Also, remember that we are trying to achieve a convincing sound of impact with an absolute minimum of force, much like what occurs when we applaud. The action is very controlled and relaxed. The head of the victim must remain relaxed to "give" a bit with the impact of the slap, thus further diminishing the force of the slap and increasing its drama. However, the victim should be careful not to respond too soon to the slap and thus increase the likelihood that the attacker will miss altogether or that the victim's ear will move into the path of the slap. Responding too soon usually occurs because the victim does not sufficiently trust the attacker.

To break the ice, the victim should slap his or her own face first, on the same cheek that's going to be slapped. This

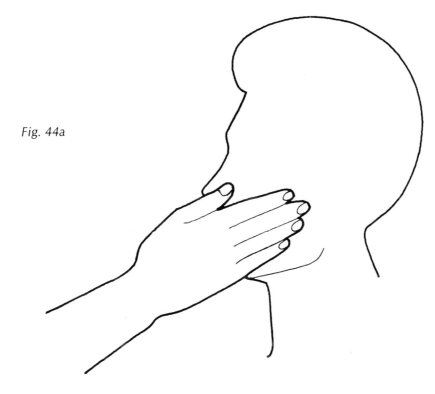

Fig. 44a

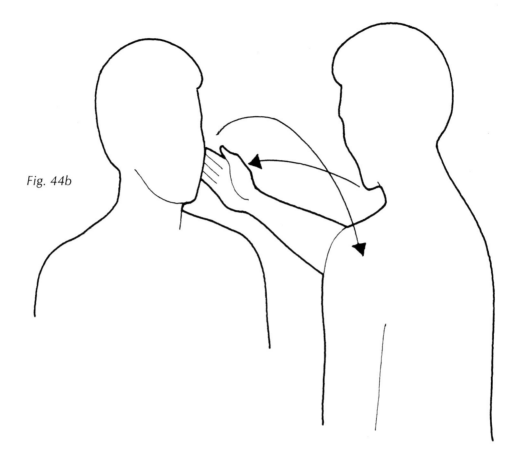

Fig. 44b

action prepares the face for the impact and also helps the attacker gauge the proper impact. The attacker should also strike his or her own cheek each and every time a contact slap is rehearsed, again to measure a comfortable striking force.

The slapping of the cheek must be practiced long before the performance, although the complete action and accurate hand placement need not end in contact every time. The attacker can repeatedly rehearse the fighting distance and swing, stopping an inch from the face, before making contact a few times. Do not overdo repetitions of a contact slap in a single session, as repeated blows will make the victim's cheek extremely sensitive.

Unfortunately, I have encountered some actors and actresses who have been told to strike the neck below the cheek because the sound is supposedly better and they are thus avoiding the eyes, ears, nose, and mouth. This is foolish and wrong! Do not strike the neck below the jaw. It is ringed by exceedingly delicate lymphatic glands, as shown in Figure 45. Moreover, the organ by which the actor makes a living — the voice box — is located in this area. And the trachea is much too vulnerably exposed to aim any kind of blow to this area of the anatomy unless you are in actual deadly earnest in order to protect your own life.

The second area of the head and neck that is fairly safe to strike is the back of the neck to either side of the spinal column. Here the primary muscle being struck is the trapezius. However, it is hard to slap the trapezius and appear to be slapping the face, and specific staging is required to create the correct illusion. In most cases, noncontact techniques are preferable.

If the following noncontact slapping techniques are performed with skill, they are extremely effective, and you need not ever actually slap a partner during a performance. Work up the noncontact slapping illusions diligently and then show them to the director. In stage combat, *seeing is believing!*

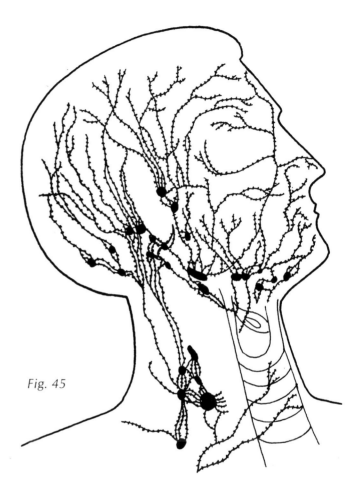

Fig. 45

Noncontact Slap 1

This slapping illusion is based entirely on placement and timing, and adheres to the safety principle: *Never cross the path of the victim's face or body.* Because this is the simplest of the slapping techniques outlined, it can be one of the most successful.

With this and the following slapping techniques, we will assume the attacker is using the right arm.

The attacker stands facing the victim forty-five degrees to the victim's left side. The attacker's right leg is slightly in advance of the left leg for stability. From this position, the attacker establishes the correct fighting distance by outstretching the right arm and standing so that the fingertips of the right hand are roughly two inches shy of making contact with the victim's face (see Figure 46 a). The attacker must be careful not to lean forward from the waist. As an attacker, you are swinging your hand with some velocity toward the path of your partner's face and so an absolutely accurate fighting distance is imperative.

The attacker then practices swinging the right arm in an arc toward the victim's face in a simulated slap, and then drawing the hand back to his or her own left shoulder (thus never crossing the path of the victim's face). The victim simultaneously jerks the head to the right, simu-

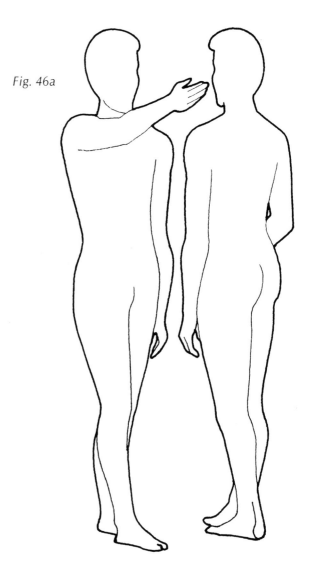

Fig. 46a

lating the reaction to the impact (see Figure 46 b).

The sound of impact (known as a *knap*) can be added by having the victim clap his or her hands (elbows close in to the body) at the exact moment when the at-

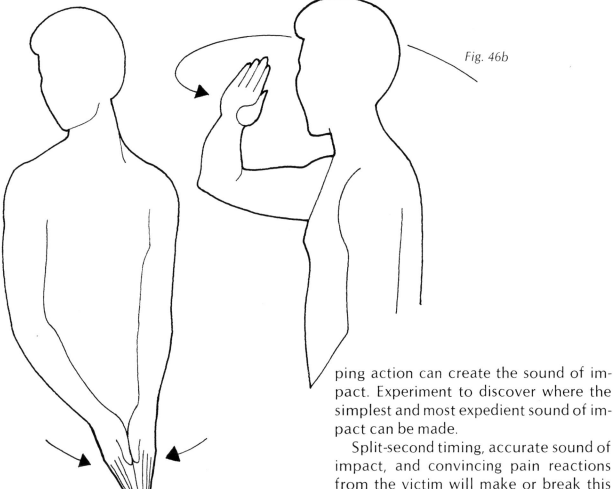

Fig. 46b

ping action can create the sound of impact. Experiment to discover where the simplest and most expedient sound of impact can be made.

Split-second timing, accurate sound of impact, and convincing pain reactions from the victim will make or break this illusion. A vocal reaction from the victim immediately following the sound of impact will greatly enhance the theatrics of this illusion and will do the same for many of the other techniques in stage combat canon. Remember, any vocal reactions of pain from the victim must come a split second *after* the sound of impact so as not to muddy the effect.

tacker's hand is parallel to the area of the victim's cheek. It is also possible for the attacker or the victim to slap a thigh with a free hand, or perhaps the sound of impact can be created by a member of an observing crowd; or a third person offstage but in close proximity to the slap-

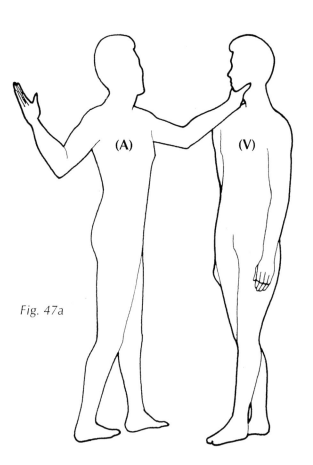

Fig. 47a

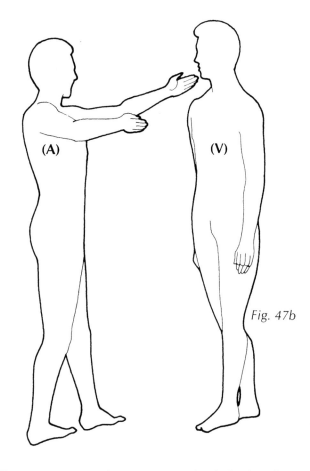

Fig. 47b

Noncontact Slap 2

This slapping technique is usually pre-ceded by a struggle of some kind, since the slap evolves out of the illusion of forcibly positioning the victim's face for the slap.

The attacker and victim stand directly facing one another, the attacker's left foot one step in advance of the right foot. The attacker places the left hand on the victim's jawline and cheek as shown in

Figure 47 a. In this position the left shoulder is slightly in advance of the right shoulder. This maneuver makes the attacker appear to position the victim's face. The attacker's left hand then is gently slipped off the victim's face by slightly bending the left elbow and pulling the left shoulder back into alignment with the right shoulder (see Figure 47b).

The left hand is then held, palm stiff and flat, directly in front of, and roughly two inches away from, the victim's face

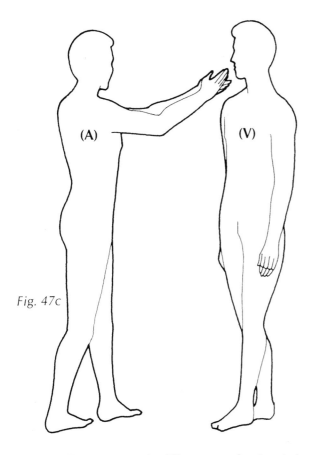

Fig. 47c

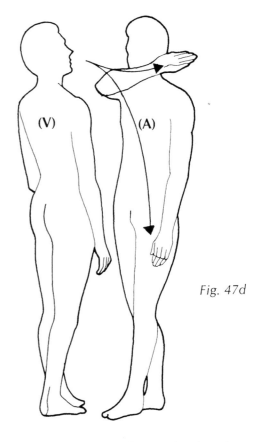

Fig. 47d

(see Figure 47 c). The attacker's right hand is simultaneously brought laterally across to strike the stiffened left hand to create the sound of impact. The attacker is in effect merely slapping his hands together in front of the victim's face. The victim of course then simulates the physical reaction to the slap.

The attacker's follow-though after the slap may prove a little difficult at first, a bit like rubbing your stomach with one hand while patting your head with the other. The attacker's left hand, after being struck by the right, immediately drops straight downward to the thigh, while the right hand, which has executed the slapping illusion, continues on its established arc from the windup, off to the attacker's left shoulder (see Figure 47 d).

Please remember that, as in the continual contact techniques, the attacker does not actually move the victim's face but relaxes and allows the victim to lead.

Noncontact Slap 3

This technique requires very accurate coordination and timing between partners. It is an essential technique to learn, however, because it can be done when one or both partners have an object in one hand.

Partners stand directly facing each other, the attacker's right foot forward, and the victim's right foot forward. From this position the victim and attacker es- tablish fighting distance. The victim bends the elbow of the right arm, places the stiffened palm of the right hand two inches directly in front of his or her own nose, and pulls the right elbow in close to the body (see Figure 48 a). Viewed from the back, the victim's body masks his or her entire right arm and hand (see Figure 48 b).

The attacker swings the right arm to the left and strikes the victim's posi- tioned right hand to simulate the slap (see

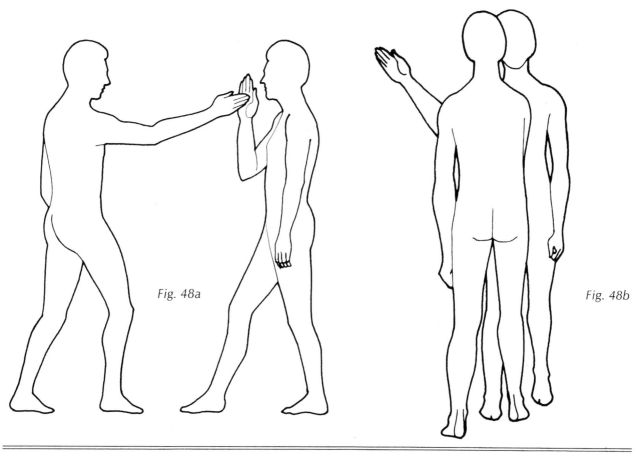

Fig. 48a

Fig. 48b

figure 48 c). The attacker follows through to the left with the right hand, while the victim's head snaps to the right. The victim may also bring the right hand to the face, covering the area of "pain" (see Figure 48 d).

The victim and the attacker must time their actions very accurately, but once perfected this action is extremely versatile.

The victim gives his or her cue for the attacker to strike. The victim's hand must be in position, fixed and stable, to assure a loud and accurate contact. The victim must avoid the urge to meet the attacker's striking hand, as this will only muddy the action.

Sometimes the victim's face and hand will naturally react to the slap as a single unit; avoid this. The head should snap to the right while the hand remains stationary; then the victim's hand either falls away or moves to the area of "pain."

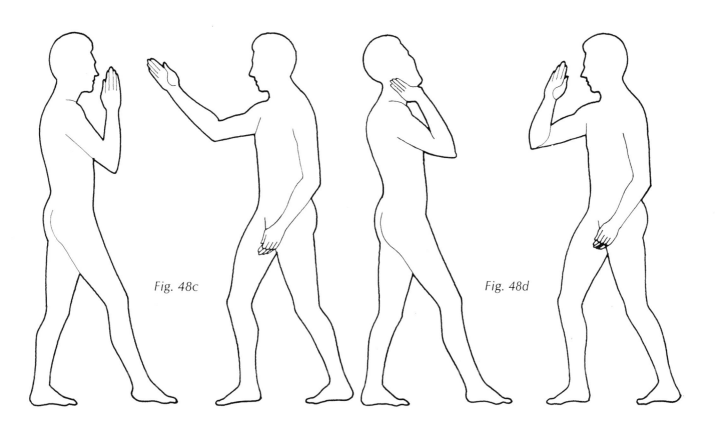

Fig. 48c

Fig. 48d

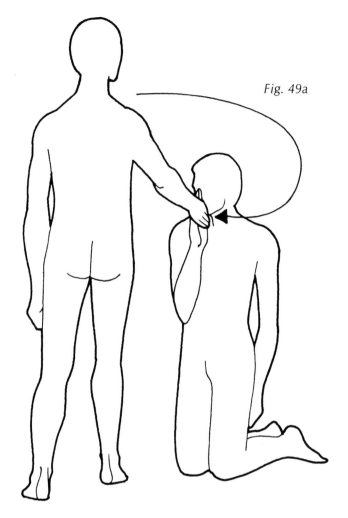

Fig. 49a

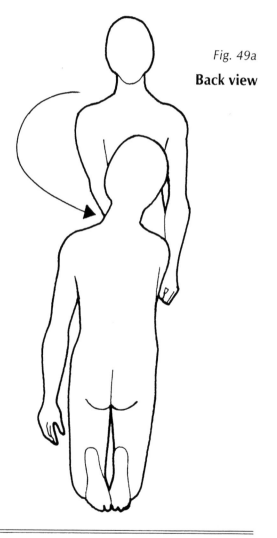

Fig. 49a

Back view

Noncontact Double Slap

This is really a variation of Noncontact Slap 3.

After the initial slap, the victim keeps the right hand rigid and snaps the head to the right (see Figure 49 a). This technique is particularly effective when the victim is kneeling directly in front of the standing attacker (see Figure 49 a, back view).

The attacker follows through and twists the wrist so that the palm of the right hand faces the victim's right side (see Figure 49 b). The attacker then slaps the backside of the victim's rigid hand as the victim's head reacts to the left (see Figure 49 c).

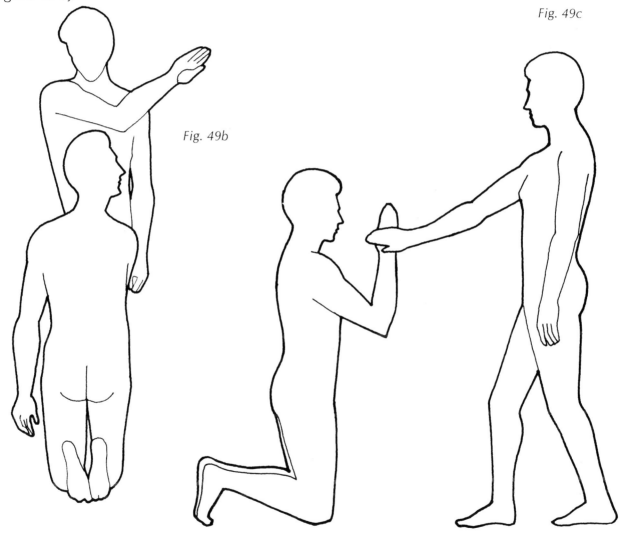

Fig. 49b

Fig. 49c

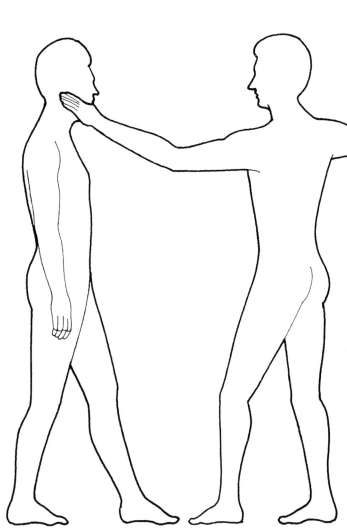

Fig. 50a

Contact Double or Triple Slap

Performing a contact slap is tricky business, requiring extreme accuracy and solid trust between combatants. Please review my comments on the pros and cons of contact slaps earlier in this chapter before you embark on learning this technique.

The attacker stands facing the victim with centerlines lined up; both have the left foot leading. The attacker begins the technique by grasping the victim's face as shown in Figure 50 a, drawing the right arm back toward the right side. The attacker takes careful aim toward the area of the victim's cheek that is safe to hit (see Contact Slap) and strikes the victim's cheek. Immediately following the impact, the attacker draws the right hand back to his own left in a follow-through, not releasing the victim's jaw with the left hand (see Figure 50 b). The attacker then strikes the back of his or her own left hand with the palm of the right hand and follows through to the right side to complete a double slap (see Figure 50 c).

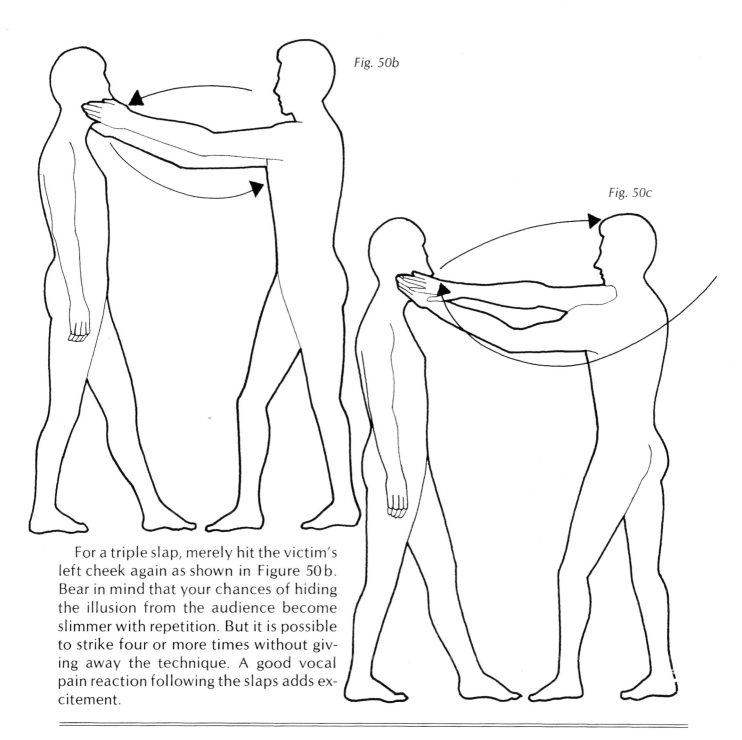

Fig. 50b

Fig. 50c

For a triple slap, merely hit the victim's left cheek again as shown in Figure 50b. Bear in mind that your chances of hiding the illusion from the audience become slimmer with repetition. But it is possible to strike four or more times without giving away the technique. A good vocal pain reaction following the slaps adds excitement.

PUNCHING

Punches have a tendency to go painfully awry because the combatants fail to allow a moment for eye contact, and because the actor or actress either forgets or doesn't believe that the punch can occur as much as six inches upstage or downstage of the victim's face and still be credible to an audience. Even at a distance of six feet, human depth perception is not entirely accurate. Add to the audience's faltering perceptions the convincing sounds of impact, split-second timing, pain reactions and perhaps some blood effects, and I can guarantee shocked gasps from the more tenderhearted observers.

Another common problem occurs when an attacker throws the entire body weight behind the punch, at the same time overextending the arm to reach the partner because the correct fighting distance was not observed. The attacker loses balance, and the moment of imbalance is a moment of lost control and a moment of potential danger.

For the instructor or director judging the proficiency of stage combatants, balance is often the key variable. Combatants should never execute choreographed techniques so fast that they lose balance, even for an instant. In addition, good balance usually indicates that the proper psychological perspective is also being maintained — i.e., the participants see the stage fight as dance and mime.

For the following punching techniques, we will assume that the attacker is using the right arm.

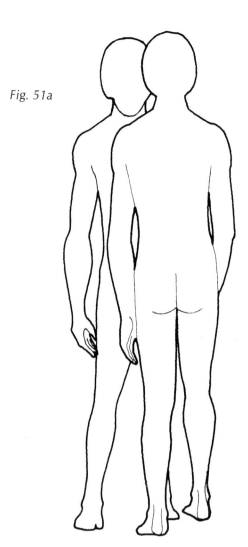

Fig. 51a

Uppercut Punch

This punching technique clearly illustrates the important rule *Never cross the path of the victim's face.* It is much too easy to actually hit your partner as a result of miscalculating fighting distance, especially in the heat of a stage fight.

The attacker stands, right foot leading, facing the victim but roughly six inches right of the victim's centerline (see Figure 51 a).

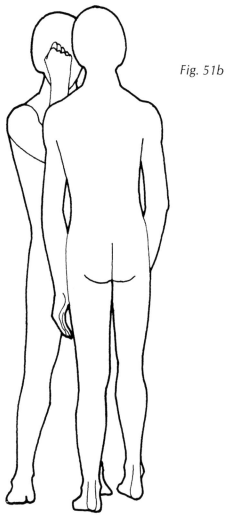

Fig. 51b

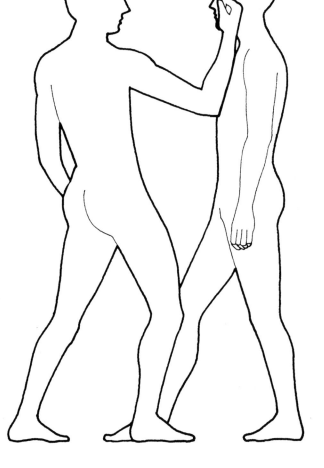

Fig. 51c

The attacker gauges the fighting distance by bending the right arm at the elbow, bringing the right fist up so it is in alignment with and six inches to the left of the victim's cheek; and then checking foot placement (see Figure 51 b). To an observer left of the attacker, the fist is hidden by the victim's face (see Figure 51 c).

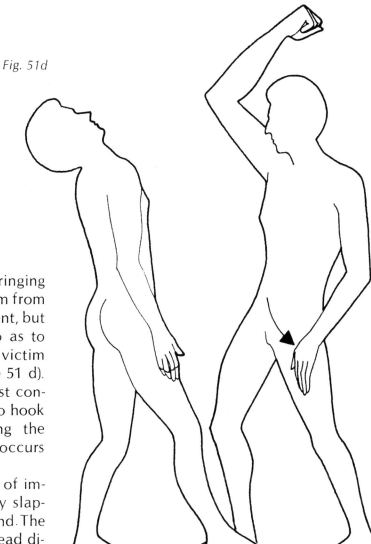

Fig. 51d

The attacker now practices bringing the fist straight up, pivoting the arm from the shoulder and with the elbow bent, but six inches to the victim's left, so as to create the illusion of clipping the victim right beneath the chin (see Figure 51 d). The attacker's follow-through must continue straight up. Be careful not to hook toward the victim's head during the follow-through, which sometimes occurs naturally.

The attacker creates the sound of impact by swiftly and surreptitiously slapping the left thigh with the left hand. The victim's reaction is to snap the head directly back, allowing the weight of the body to follow. Remember that the head goes straight backwards, not to the left or right side. The size of the windup, the speed of the uppercut punch, and the volume of the sound of impact will dictate the degree of reaction to the punch.

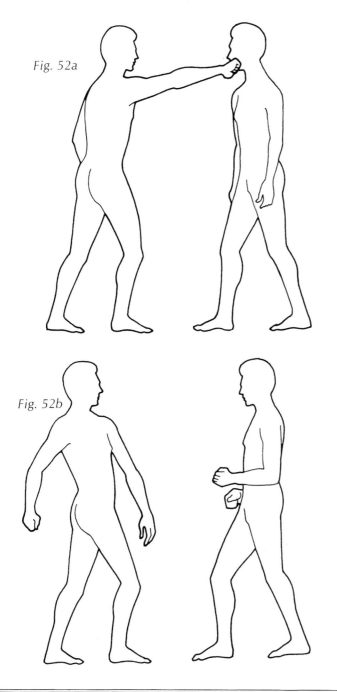

Fig. 52a

Fig. 52b

Roundhouse Punch

As this is an old favorite John Wayne punch, you have probably seen it performed many times on television and in the movies. Remember, much of the excitement is in the windup.

The attacker stands, right foot leading, facing the victim. The attacker gauges the fighting distance by extending the punching arm so that the fist is at least two inches to one side of the victim's face at the supposed point of impact (see Figure 52 a).

For the windup, the attacker brings the right fist back and slightly down toward the right hip (see Figure 52 b). The attacker then swings the fist toward the victim's face. When it is about two inches from, and to the left side of, the victim's face, the attacker pulls the fist toward his or her own left shoulder (see Figures 52 c and 52 d), thus describing an approximate 180-degree arc to and away from the victim's face.

The victim's first reaction is to snap the head and face away from the fist, in alignment with the arc of the attacker's swing (see Figure 52 e). The victim's body weight then follows.

Either the attacker or victim may add the sound of impact by slapping the upstage thigh at the exact moment when the fist reaches the side of the victim's face.

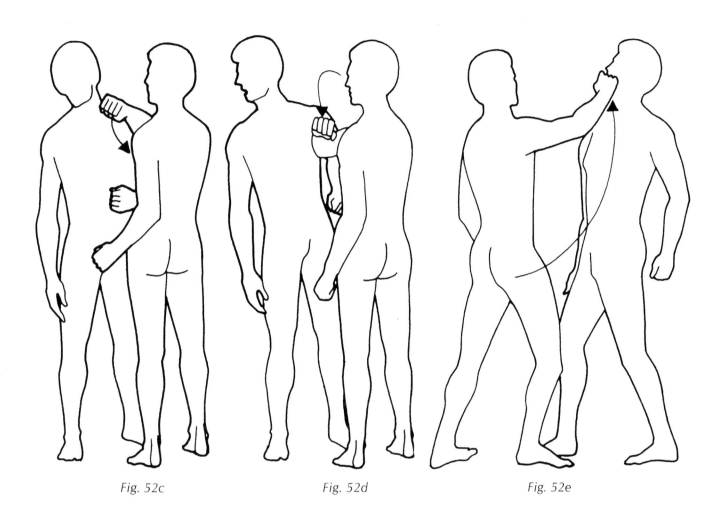

Fig. 52c   Fig. 52d   Fig. 52e

Jab

The straight jab is an extremely simple illusion, but it can help an actor portray an experienced fighter since it is associated with professional boxing.

The attacker stands, right foot leading, facing the victim. The fist is shot straight from the shoulder, and in actual boxing it travels in a straight line to the chin or eye. In stage combat, however, the fist is two or three inches left of the victim's face (see Figure 53 a). The attacker's fist once again never crosses the path of the victim's face.

The victim's head snaps directly back from the illusory impact, with the weight of the body following (see Figure 53 b). The victim should take it easy on the head reaction to this punch, as generally the neck muscles involved are weak and easily become stiffened and sore.

The sound of impact is made by either the attacker slapping his chest or the victim slapping his or her thigh at the moment of supposed impact (see Figure 53 c). The chest or thigh slap must be quick and hard, producing a sharp crack.

As in the other striking techniques, follow four steps in learning the routine: (1) establish fighting distance; (2) practice the actions out of distance; (3) practice within distance in slow motion; (4) slowly speed up the illusion to performance level.

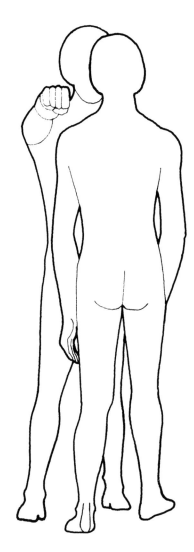

Fig. 53a

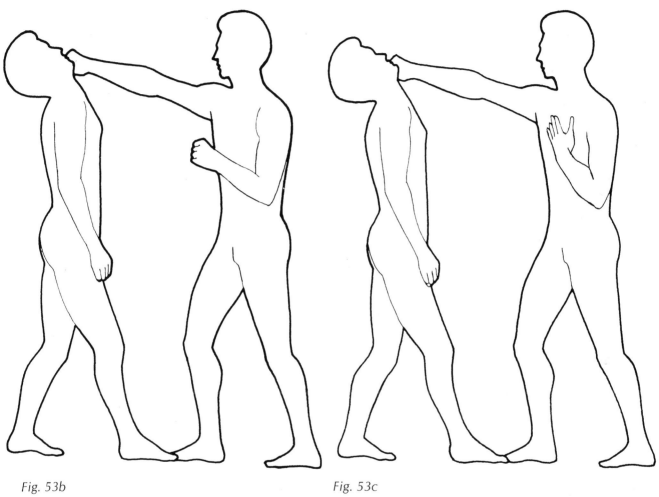

Fig. 53b

Fig. 53c

Backhand Punch

This technique is not often used, and so it holds a particularly vicious surprise for the audience.

The attacker stands with the right foot on the outside of the victim's right foot; thus the attacker's centerline is far to the right of the victim's centerline (see Figure 54 a).

As the name implies, the supposed contact is made by the back of a closed fist. Therefore, the windup begins as the attacker places the right fist (palm downward) at the left hip (see Figure 54 b).

The fighting distance is ascertained by the attacker extending the right arm so

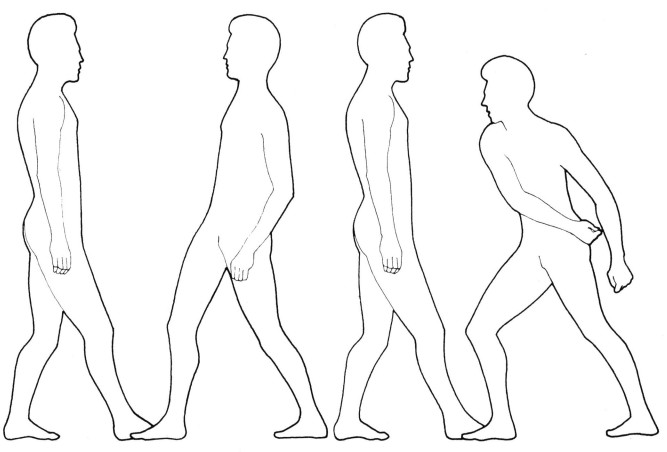

Fig. 54a   Fig. 54b

that the right fist is parallel to, and two inches away from, the victim's right cheek (see Figure 54 c).

The attacker's fist travels almost directly straight up, past, and always to the outside of the victim's face. The attacker's fist remains on the victim's right side throughout the action.

The victim reacts by snapping the head back and to the left, with the body weight following. The attacker follows through by extending the right arm straight up in the air (see Figure 54 d).

The sound of impact is created by the attacker slapping the left thigh with the left hand. Of course the victim may also create the sound of impact by slapping the upstage thigh.

Fig. 54c   Fig. 54d

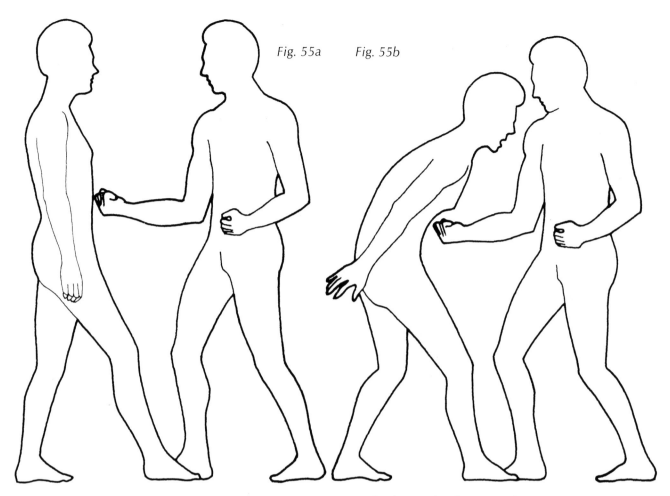

Fig. 55a   *Fig. 55b*

Stomach Punch

Many an audience member has been certain that this punch is a gimmick, but the doubters have yet to discover what that may be.

This technique also relies heavily on a loud sound of impact and a proper physical reaction. Basically, the reaction is the victim's explosion of vocalized breath.

The attacker stands facing the victim, with the right foot leading. The fighting distance is established by having the attacker extend the right arm so that the fist (palm facing upwards) is two inches shy of the victim's stomach (see Figure 55 a). Note that the attacker's right arm is bent at the elbow, not fully extended; this aids the illusion that the fist is being stopped by the mass of the victim's body. There is no follow-through as there is with the facial punches.

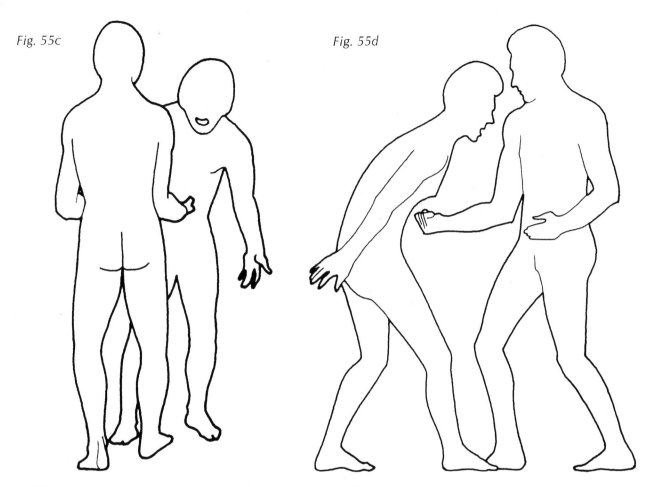

Fig. 55c

Fig. 55d

The attacker practices the windup and punch (Figure 55 b), and the victim simultaneously practices the contraction that results from a blow to the stomach (see Figure 55 c). The victim should be careful that the final position does not give the impression that the punch was to the chest. The victim should lower the head to the right or left during the reaction — not directly forward and into the attacker's nose.

The attacker creates the sound of impact by hitting his or her own tensed stomach muscles with the left open palm simultaneously with the punch (see Figure 55 d).

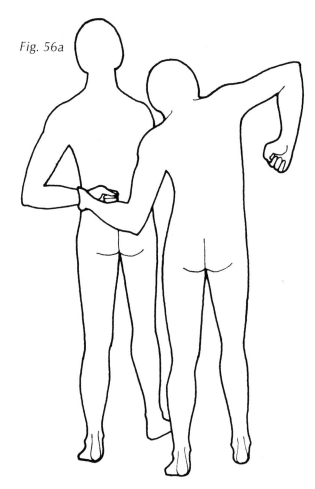

Fig. 56a

Kidney Punch

This is a more specialized technique that requires a transitional movement to allow the attacker to get behind the victim. The illusion of bending an arm behind the victim's back might be a good lead-in technique for this punch.

The attacker stands, right foot leading, behind the victim, whose right foot is also leading. The attacker holds the victim's left arm behind the back with the left hand. Since the attacker is behind the victim, eye contact cannot be made. Establish a physical cue. For example, the attacker may squeeze the victim's wrist twice rapidly before each punch.

The attacker makes a fist with the right hand and winds up for the punch by cocking the right arm directly back, as in the wind-up for the uppercut or stomach punch (see Figure 56 a).

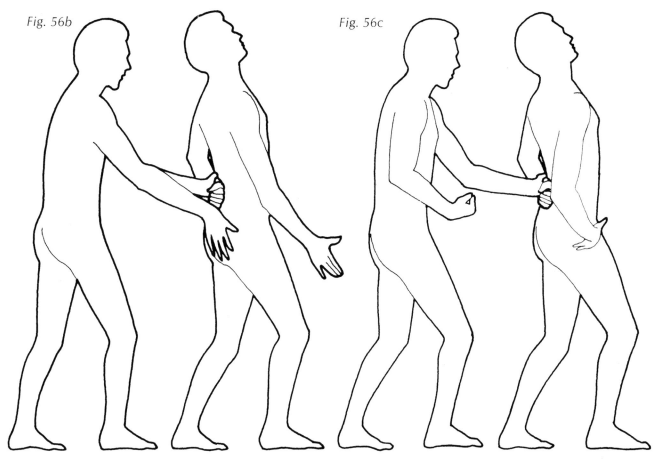

Fig. 56b

Fig. 56c

The attacker's fist swings to within roughly five inches of the victim's back. Then the attacker opens the hand and bends the wrist, so as to flatten the palm and heel of the right hand. This action is hidden from the audience by the victim's and the attacker's bodies. The attacker then strikes the victim on the rump with the open right hand (see Figure 56b). The attacker must be very careful not to strike the victim's middle or lower back but to hit the right gluteus maximus muscle.

The attacker immediately brings the right hand back, as in a recoil, but with the hand again clenched into a fist (see Figure 56 c). Thus the audience assumes that the hand was closed in a fist the whole time. It does take a little practice to coordinate the opening and closing of the attacker's fist; so be patient and don't rush this technique.

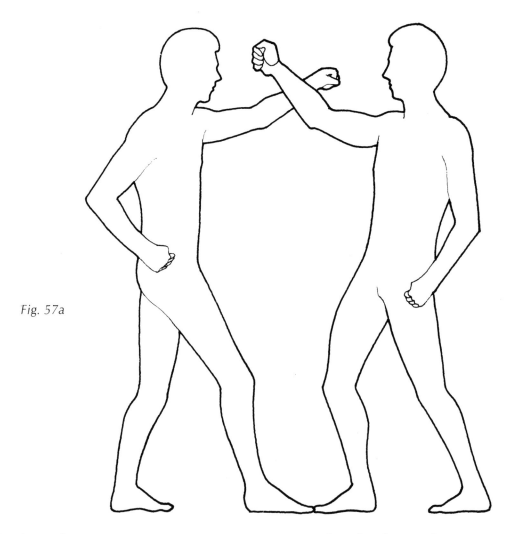

Fig. 57a

Block and Punch

This was an indispensable technique for the fight arrangers of the old film westerns. You may find it just as necessary.

The attacker stands, right foot leading, facing the victim. The victim's right foot is also leading. The victim throws a Roundhouse Punch with the left arm, which is blocked by the attacker's right forearm (see Figure 57 a). The victim's roundhouse and attacker's block must be spatially choreographed so that they meet rather than clash together as they would in an actual fight. This precaution

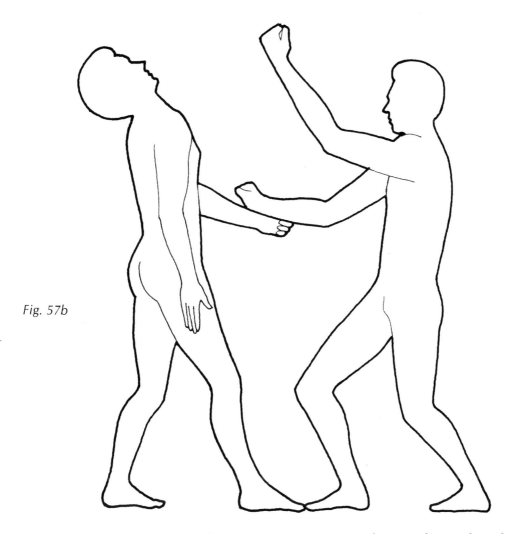

Fig. 57b

not only saves the arms when the technique is continually repeated in practice, but also develops the special awareness, akin to mime, that is the physical realm of stage combat as opposed to street fighting.

The attacker then throws an Uppercut Punch by bending the right knee and swinging the "striking" fist directly upwards (see Figure 57 b). (A Jab, Roundhouse, or Stomach Punch could also be used.)

The victim makes the sound of impact by slapping the left thigh with the left hand.

Elbow Jab

This is an interesting and effective technique for the victim to use as an escape from a Forearm Choke or an armlock from behind. In this version, the victim, who is about to experience an Elbow Jab, has the attacker in a Forearm Choke and is very close to the attacker's body (see Figure 58 a). The attacker brings the right arm forward for the windup (see Figure 58 b). The attacker brings the right arm directly back and slaps the inside of the upper arm against his or her own body; this creates the sound of impact (Figure 58 c). And since the striking elbow does not pass beyond the attacker's body, the victim is protected from an accidental poke with the elbow.

The knap can also be made by the attacker or victim striking a thigh with a free hand.

The attacker heightens the illusion of impacting against the victim's body by tightening the muscles of the trunk and striking arm.

The victim then vocalizes a grunt, simultaneously releases the attacker, and mimes the pain reactions of a blow to the ribs.

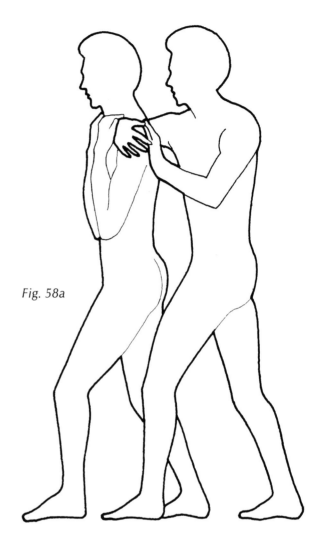

Fig. 58a

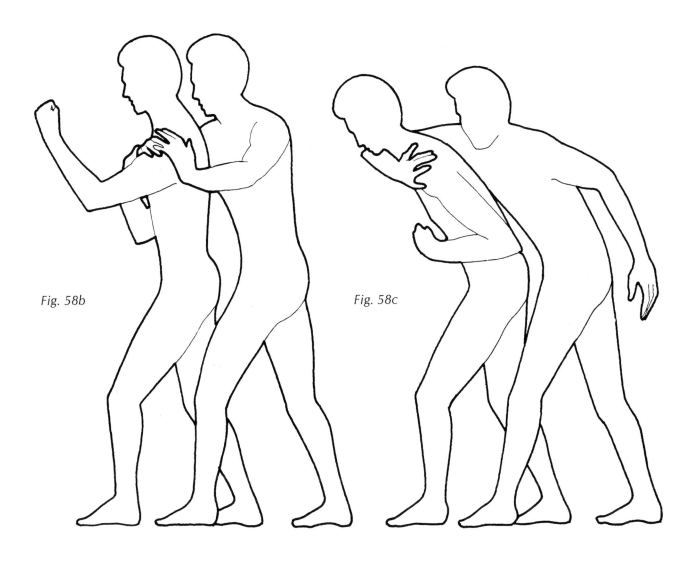

Fig. 58b

Fig. 58c

Cross Jab 1

Another favorite of John Wayne! This version of the jab violates the precaution of never crossing the path of the victim's face. Therefore I suggest introducing it only after the ordinary Jab has been mastered.

The attacker stands directly opposite the victim. William Hobbs, a leading fight choreographer in Great Britain, suggests gauging fighting distance by extending the left arm, if punching with the right, as though setting up the victim for the punch (see Figure 59 a). You'll see John Wayne do this quite often in his fights.

The attacker's right hand, shaped into a fist, crosses to the victim's right shoulder. The fist opens up into a flat palm which strikes the victim's shoulder (see Figure 59 b). The attacker's striking hand closes immediately after impact into a fist again, to maintain the illusion. The victim reacts to the right as though struck in the face.

The knap is created by the impact of the attacker's open palm on the victim's shoulder.

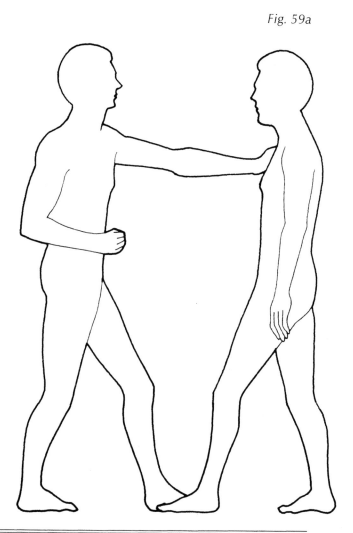

Fig. 59a

Cross Jab 2

To begin this variation, the attacker grabs the victim's right shoulder with the left hand as in Cross Jab 1 (Figure 59 a). The attacker then swings with a closed fist across to the victim's right shoulder, slightly below the level of the victim's chin. At the last possible moment the attacker releases the victim, turns the left palm towards the right fist, and strikes the open left palm with the right fist (see Figure 60). This blow creates the sound of impact.

The victim twists the face to the right, tilts the head back, looks pained, and cries out.

Fig. 59b

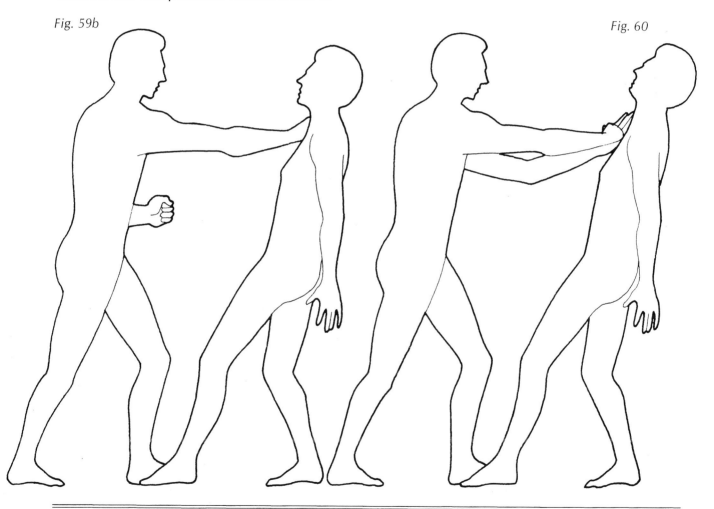

Fig. 60

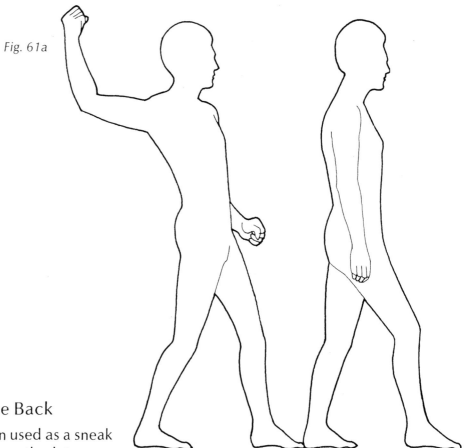

Fig. 61a

Hammer Punch to the Back

This technique is often used as a sneak attack. I've see Bruce Lee, the late martial artist and film actor, silently sneak up on an unsuspecting sentry and strike him "unconscious" with a hammer punch to the back of the neck!

The attacker stands behind the victim with the left foot leading. In lieu of eye contact, the attacker cues the victim by using the left foot to touch the victim's heel. The attacker simultaneously raises his or her right hand, clenched into a fist, above the head (see Figure 61 a).

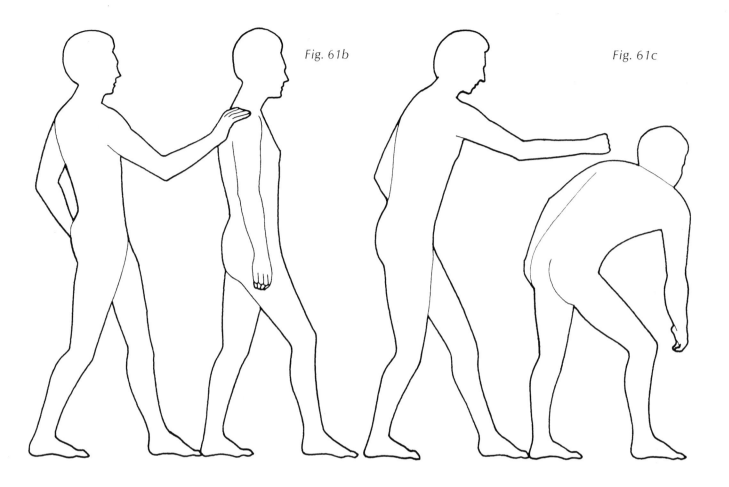

Fig. 61b

Fig. 61c

The attacker brings the right fist down toward the victim's right shoulder, as though performing a hammer blow to the back of the victim's neck, but instead the attacker opens the right fist and slaps the victim's right shoulder with an open palm, creating the sound of impact (see Figure 61 b).

The victim responds by collapsing down and away from the point of contact and adds a vocal reaction following the sound of impact.

The attacker draws the right hand immediately back from the open palm blow and again forms a fist (see Figure 61 c). This fist-palm-fist action happens so quickly that the audience only sees the attacker's closed fist.

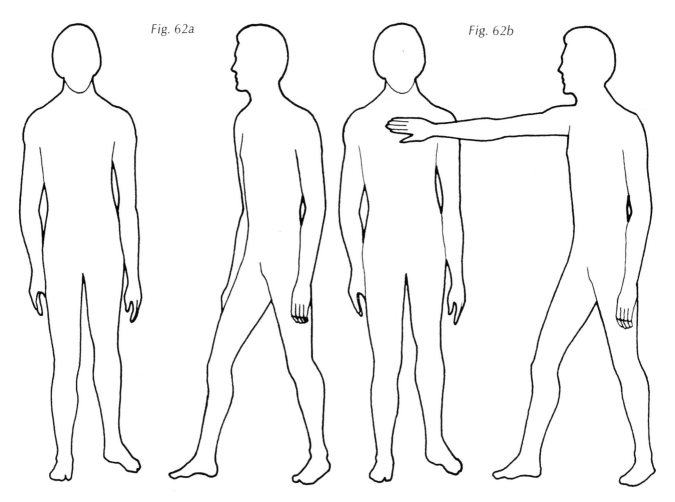

Fig. 62a

Fig. 62b

Karate "Knife Hand" to the Throat

This is another particularly vicious illusion, appropriate only for combatants playing characters who are seasoned fighters.

The preparatory position is very important to this technique to maximize the sound of the impact and for the audience to observe the illusion. The attacker stands to the victim's left, with both the attacker's and victim's right legs leading (see Figure 62 a).

At proper fighting distance, the attacker is able to place the right open palm on the victim's upper chest without bending at the waist or stepping forward, as illustrated in Figure 62b.

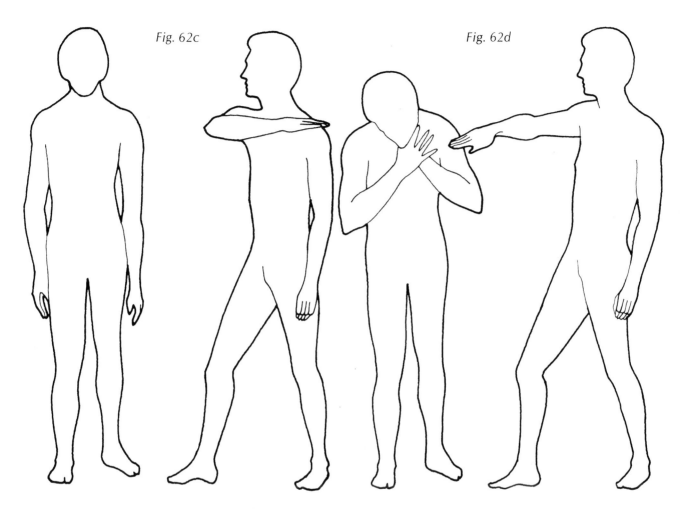

Fig. 62c   Fig. 62d

The attacker winds up by drawing his or her right arm back toward the left shoulder and forming a "knife hand" with the outside edge of the palm facing the victim (see Figure 62 c). This hand slices through the air towards the victim. Just before making contact, the attacker turns the palm towards the victim and loudly slaps the victim's upper chest. The hand immediately rebounds and turns back on edge, so that the audience believes it has never left that position. The victim responds as though having been struck in the throat (see Figure 62d).

KNEEING, KICKING, AND STOMPING

Because kneeing, kicking, and stomping are associated with a vicious commitment to violence, these techniques are particularly effective with audiences and can be used as climactic moments within a fight. However, you'll find them to be very good transitional moves as well.

Approach the following techniques with more than your customary caution. I have found that performers do not have as much kinesthetic awareness of their leg movements as they do of arm movements. Also, the leg can be a bit more difficult to control than the arm, since the combatant is maintaining balance on one leg while swinging the considerable weight of the other leg.

Again, I cannot stress enough the importance of eye contact preceding every illusion. Remember that eye contact is the moment the partners take to look into each other's eyes as a signal that the illusion is about to take place. Eye contact is maintained only for a brief interval, after which the combatants immediately look to the points of contact for the illusion.

It is also important to pay very special attention to the fighting distance. It will vary with the technique and the length of the performers' legs.

With the kneeing, kicking, and stomping techniques — as indeed with all combat mime situations — the name of the game is adjustment and compromise. Be totally concerned with your partner's needs and well-being. Once the two of you have established the technique, you must repeat, repeat, and repeat again. When concentration begins to drift, rest for a few moments.

Knee in Face

This is a good barroom brawl technique.

The attacker faces the victim and raises the right knee with the left foot forward and in alignment with the victim's centerline. The attacker places the left hand on the back of the victim's head and the right hand on the victim's left shoulder (see Figure 63 a).

Practicing in slow motion, the victim brings the head down, while the attacker brings the right knee up to the left outside of the victim's face and head. As the victim's head is descending, the attacker slides both hands off the victim and brings the right hand down with a slapping motion to the thigh of the raised leg (see Figure 63 b), thus creating the sound of impact.

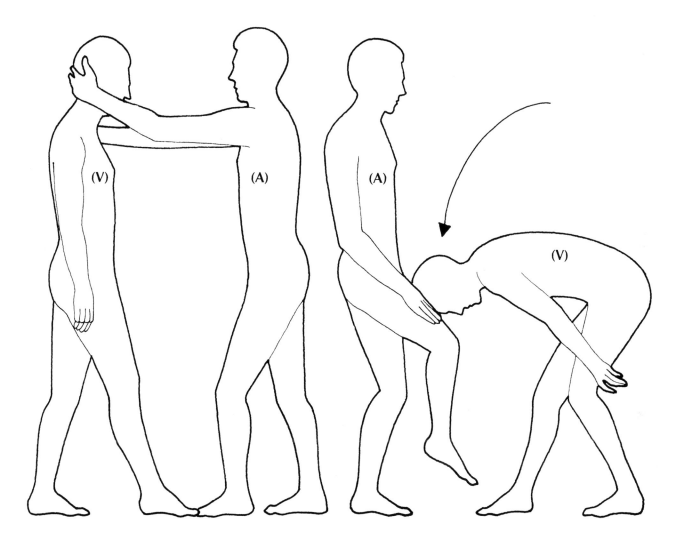

Fig. 63a

Fig. 63b

The victim then allows the head to whip back as though rebounding from the attacker's knee. The victim may also bring both hands up to cover the face, strengthening the illusion (see Figure 63 c).

The attacker must not pull at all on the victim's head. Remember, the victim initiates the pain-inflicting action, while the attacker merely follows. The attacker must be extremely sure to bring the knee up to the outside of the victim's face and head.

Preceding the practice of this technique, the partner who is the attacker must practice lifting the knee while maintaining balance until the move becomes second nature. Having a sure balance will help the attacker avoid falling into the victim or depending upon the victim's body to maintain balance.

Another variation that is just as simple is to have the attacker place both hands on either side of the victim's head, reinforcing the illusion that the attacker is pulling the victim's head toward the knee. In this variation the sound of impact is created by the attacker slapping the raised thigh with both hands.

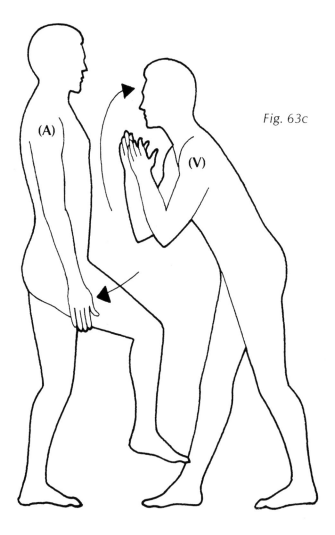

Fig. 63c

Knee in Groin

This is entirely a mimed technique. The attacker's knee does not contact the victim's groin, and the effect is largely created by the victim's pain reactions.

The attacker stands directly in front of the victim and places both hands on the victim's shoulders. The attacker's supporting leg is slightly leading the leg that will be lifted for the kneeing action (see Figure 64 a).

The attacker places both hands on the victim's shoulders for steadiness during the action. An attacker who has completed the technique as outlined many, many times may vary this technique by placing only one hand on the victim's shoulder, or perhaps by improvising a mock struggle with the attacker holding the victim's wrists preceding the kneeing action.

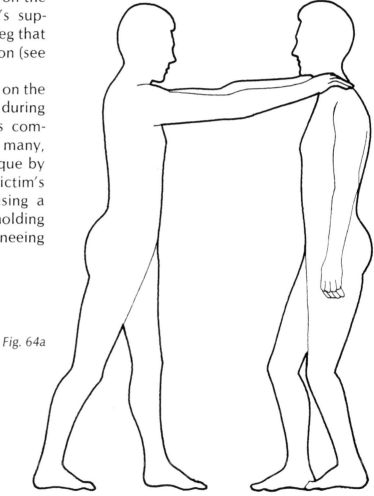

Fig. 64a

The attacker receives eye contact, then looks down and lifts the right knee, bringing it up to within roughly three inches of the victim's right inner thigh (see Figure 64 b). Note that I did not say to stop short of the *groin* but the *right inner thigh.* The attacker's focus is not the victim's groin, but the thigh. I trust you can readily see that this is an obvious and important distinction.

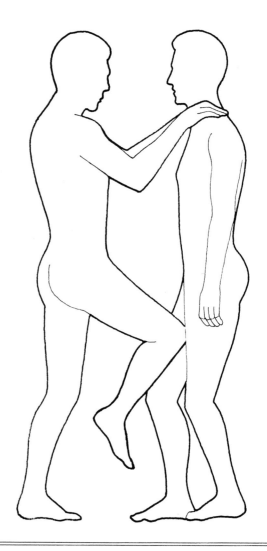

Fig. 64b

Either the attacker or the victim may make the sound of impact by striking a heavy, fleshy area, such as a buttock or thigh, to create a thudding slap. In this example, the victim creates the sound of impact by striking the thigh (see Figure 64 c). Of course the sound of impact must be executed away from the audience's view and with a snap of the wrist, not a large, swinging arm movement, which could destroy the illusion.

Immediately following the sound of impact, the victim bends over, contracting toward the pelvis, at the same time exhaling and groaning. The attacker should remain upright and not bend sympathetically with the victim, which occasionally occurs.

Please practice the raising of the knee to the victim's inner thigh in slow motion many times. You are not allowed any mistakes in this technique.

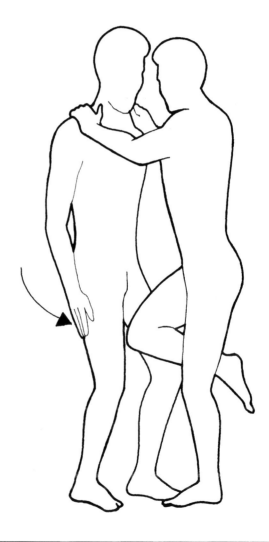

Fig. 64c

Knee in Stomach

The attacker stands to the victim's left side, so that the planes of the two partners' bodies form a right angle. The attacker then places the left hand on the victim's left shoulder and the right hand on the victim's left hip, for stability (see Figure 65 a).

The victim turns the head upstage and establishes eye contact with the attacker (see Figure 65 b).

The attacker raises the right knee at the same time that the victim bends over from the waist. The attacker's right knee stops short of hitting the victim in the stomach (not the chest) (see Figure 65 c).

A vocal reaction from the victim is usually enough, but the victim or the attacker can supply a knap if desired. Either the victim can hit his or her upstage thigh, or the attacker can strike his or her own hidden thigh with the right hand. Remember that the knap precedes any vocal reactions.

The attacker must be able to balance without the support of the victim. The attacker must not rise on the ball of the supporting foot when the knee rises but must keep the entire supporting foot flat on the floor.

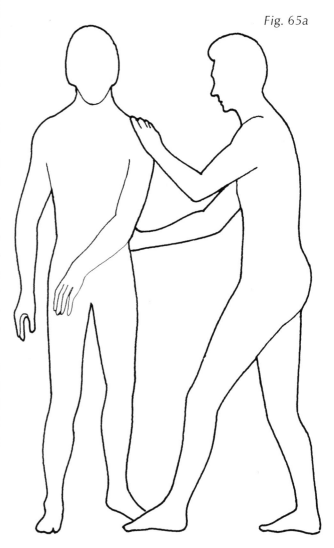

Fig. 65a

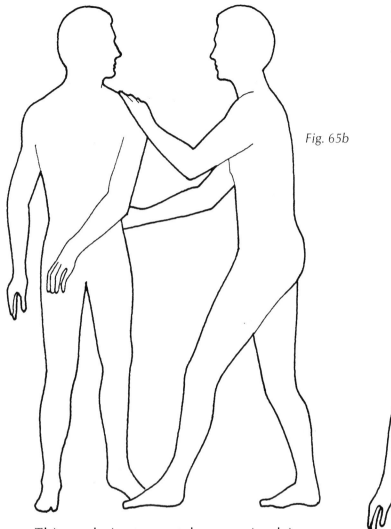

Fig. 65b

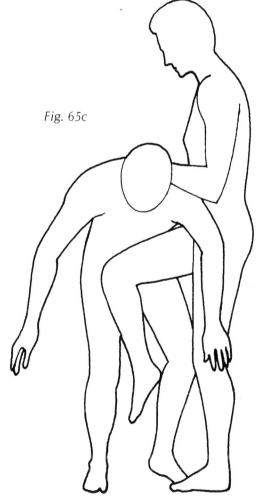

Fig. 65c

This technique must be practiced in slow motion many times to establish how far the attacker should raise the knee to create the illusion without striking the victim. The victim must in turn learn how to bend down without striking the attacker's knee.

Stomach Kick

This illusion is very effective for ending a fight; it might also be used to seemingly break the taboo against kicking a woman in the stomach. After all, violence is not a subject to be shaped by good taste. Let it never be our intention to make violence acceptable to an audience, or we will do a moral disservice to our community. In a naturalistic or realistic theatrical context, violence should horrify. Be clear on style and intention, and let us differentiate violence from slapstick.

The Stomach Kick is an entirely mimed technique. No contact is made between the attacker and the victim.

Initially, the victim kneels on all fours, and the attacker approaches the victim from the side (see Figure 66 a). The attacker then gauges fighting distance so that his or her extended, not flexed, kicking foot is hidden beneath the victim's body at the supposed point of contact, the stomach (see Figure 66 b). The attacker must be careful not to accidentally kick the victim in the ribs with his or her shin bone, and this may happen if fighting distance is too short.

The attacker winds up by drawing back the kicking leg. The attacker then swings

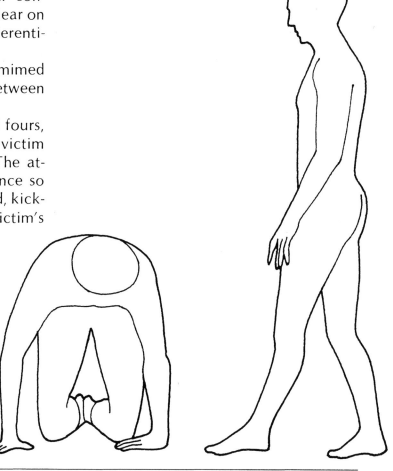

Fig. 66a

the leg (foot extended) toward the victim and stops the forward motion of the leg when the foot is beneath the victim's stomach. At this moment, the attacker should contract all muscles isometrically in order to create the illusion that the foot has been stopped by a heavy object: the body of the victim.

Just as the impact supposedly occurs, the victim should tighten the stomach muscles and lurch up just a bit. There should also be a convincing vocal reaction from the victim, which may be enough in itself to make this technique effective. However, the illusion is most powerful when a knap precedes a vocal reaction. The attacker may create a sound of impact by slapping his or her stomach or thigh (see Figure 66 c). The victim may also create the knap by striking his or her hidden thigh.

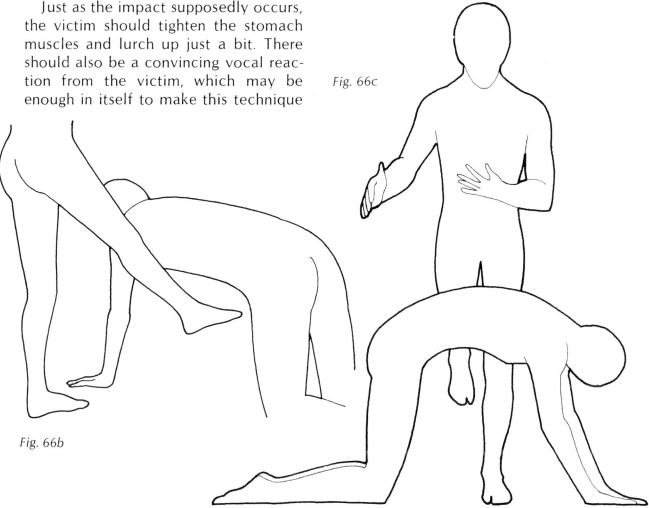

Fig. 66c

Fig. 66b

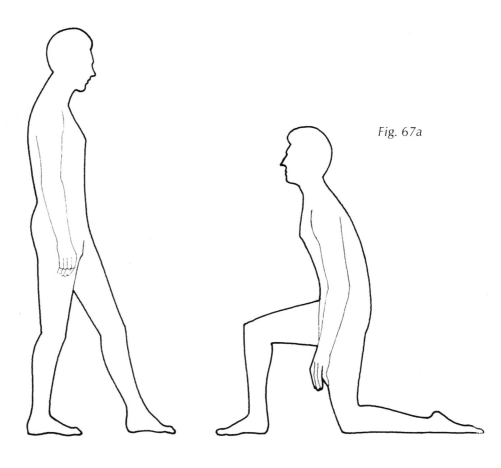

Simple Face Kick

This is another entirely mimed technique: the attacker and victim make no physical contact whatsoever.

The victim kneels on the left knee facing the attacker and bends slightly forward from the waist. The attacker stands facing the victim, so that the leading left foot is in alignment with the victim's centerline (see Figure 67 a).

The attacker winds up by bringing the right leg back, then swings the right leg forward and extends it to the left side of the victim's face (over the victim's left shoulder). Seen from the side, the attacker's right foot lines up with the victim's left cheek (see Figure 67 b).

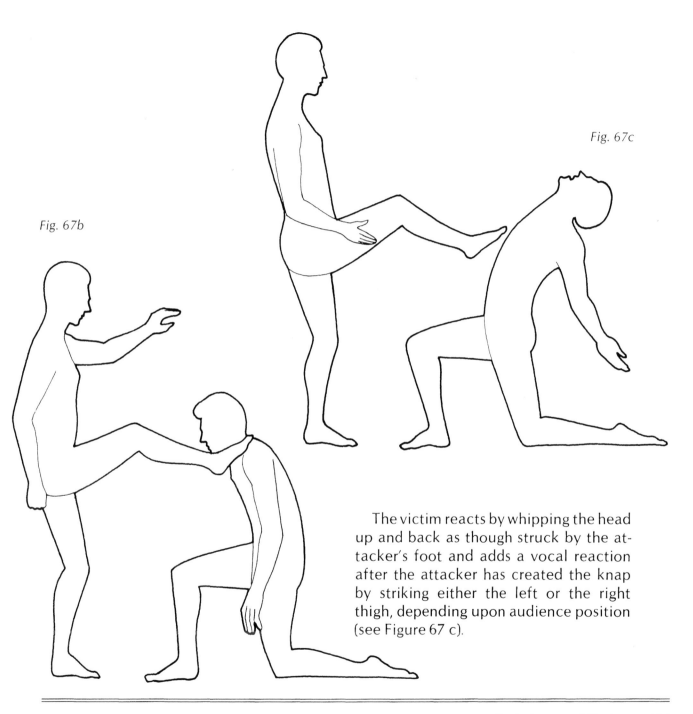

Fig. 67b

Fig. 67c

The victim reacts by whipping the head up and back as though struck by the attacker's foot and adds a vocal reaction after the attacker has created the knap by striking either the left or the right thigh, depending upon audience position (see Figure 67 c).

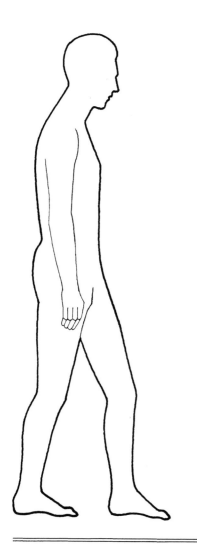

Instep Face Kick

When this technique is accurately timed and executed, I think it is easily one of the most spectacular combat mime illusions.

The following directions are for a kick with the right foot. They need merely be reversed for lefties.

The victim kneels on the left knee, bending slightly forward at the waist. The right arm is held across the face and the right hand is stretched beyond the left shoulder, presenting a flat, firm target for the attacker (see Figure 68 a).

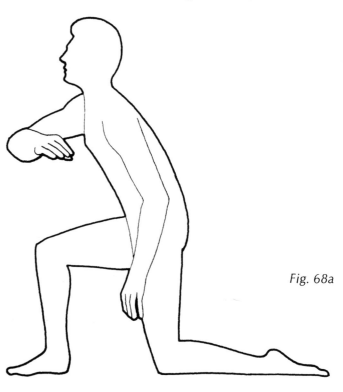

Fig. 68a

The attacker stands facing the victim with the left foot directly in alignment with the victim's centerline.

Before performing the next action, the attacker must perfect a kick that is very light, yet firm enough to make a sound.

The impact is similar to that of a hand clap, because the attacker is going to strike the victim's hand with the flat portion of the instep.

Although the entire right leg is brought back for the wind up, the kick pivots from the knee (see Figure 68 b). The kicking foot should be a comfortable distance from the victim's hand so as to reach it without causing imbalance through overextension.

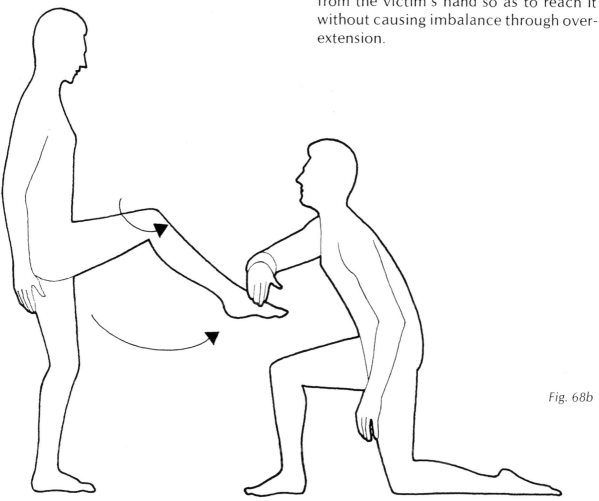

Fig. 68b

Practice the kicking as an isolated exercise before incorporating it into the illusion. Next, position the victim's hand to the height of the attacker's comfortable kick. Both partners must work together so that the attacker will not be imbalanced by attempting to kick too high and the victim is not so low that eye contact is difficult to establish.

A split second after the attacker's foot has made the sound of impact, the victim's head reacts by jerking up and back, thus carrying the weight of the body after the head (see Figure 68 c). The attacker remains motionless for a moment so that the audience can view the attacker's extended rigid leg juxtaposed to the vic-

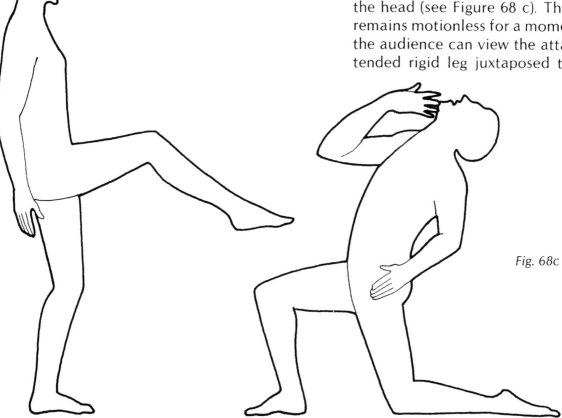

Fig. 68c

tim's reaction backwards. Please also note that the victim's right hand, which receives the impact, should not be allowed to rebound too high from the kick, or the audience will perceive the trick behind the illusion.

A variation on this face kick sometimes gives the victim more confidence. In this variation the centerlines of the victim and attacker line up. The victim uses both hands to receive the kick. The right hand is over the left hand and the palm of the left hand is angled toward the ground to receive the instep of the attacker's kicking foot (see Figure 68 d). After the impact, kicking foot striking the victim's left palm, the victim reacts backwards.

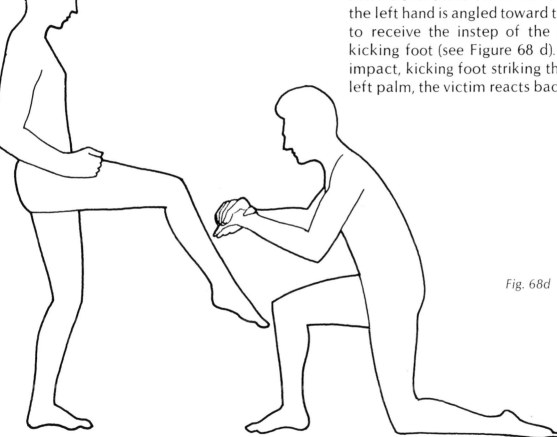

Fig. 68d

Standing Contact Groin Kick 1

Do the groin kicks need an introduction?

The victim stands with one foot well in advance of the other. In this instance the victim's right leg is leading because the attacker is more comfortable kicking with the right foot. The attacker stands facing his or her partner with the left foot leading (see Figure 69 a).

Fighting distance depends on the length of the attacker's leg and by the placement of the attacker's instep on the back of the victim's thigh. The attacker will be kicking the inside thigh of the victim's leading right leg with the flat portion of the instep of the right foot (see Figure 69 b). The attacker must never allow the toe to strike the thigh as this can be quite painful. A firm but controlled kick with the instep is called for; point the toe and don't flex the foot. The attacker must use as little force as possible to create the knap. Control is directly related to balance. Don't hurry; practice step by step.

The attacker's supporting foot is pivoted ninety degrees so that it is parallel to the victim. This position helps the attacker shift the hips and twist the knee so as to kick horizontally. If the foot travels horizontally, it will not slide higher toward the groin. A flat, not angled, instep is presented to the heavy back portion of the victim's thigh.

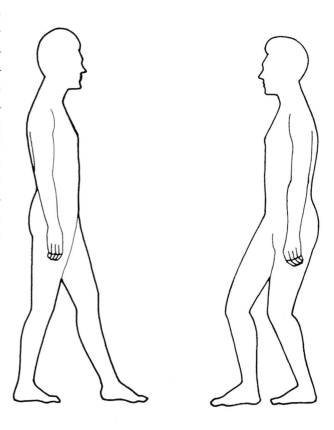

Fig. 69a

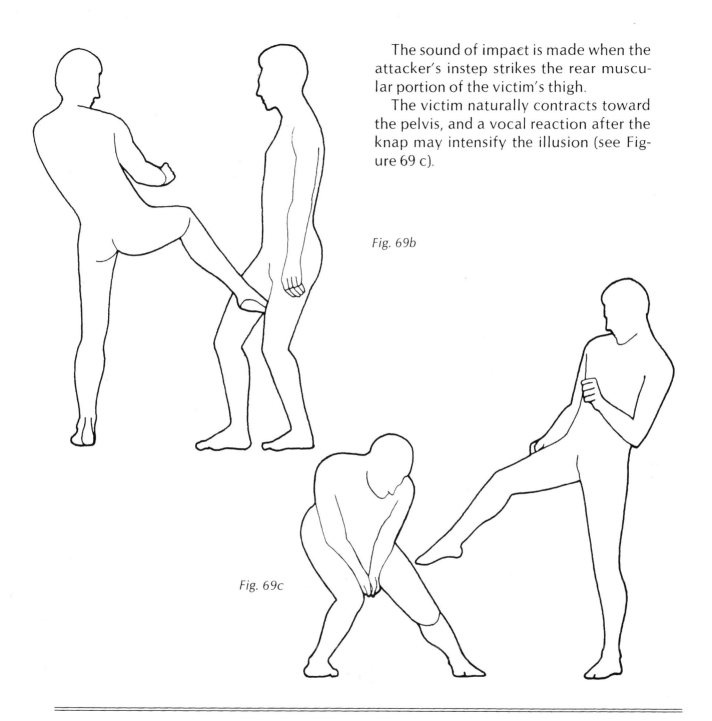

The sound of impact is made when the attacker's instep strikes the rear muscular portion of the victim's thigh.

The victim naturally contracts toward the pelvis, and a vocal reaction after the knap may intensify the illusion (see Figure 69 c).

Fig. 69b

Fig. 69c

Standing Contact Groin Kick 2

At the risk of seeming indelicate, I will remind my readers that men should wear a dance belt or athletic supporter when practicing and performing this variation.

This technique demands a great deal of control with the kicking leg. A novice fighter should learn Standing Contact Groin Kick 1 before using this version. However, variation 2 can be extremely effective for in-the-round, or arena, staging.

If the attacker is kicking with the right leg, he or she stands with the left leg to the outside of the victim's right leg (see Figure 70 a).

The kick occurs between the victim's legs, with the instep of the attacker's foot hitting the victim's right buttock well to the right of the spine (see Figure 70 b). This blow creates the sound of impact. Of course the victim responds to the kick with a vocal reaction following the impact, and contracts as shown in Figure 69c.

Fig. 70a

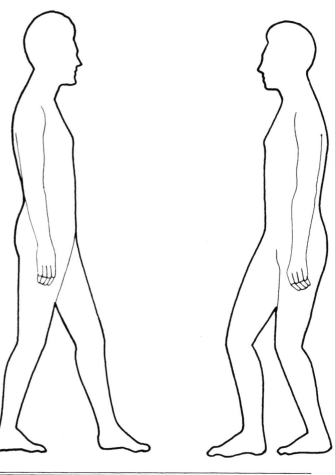

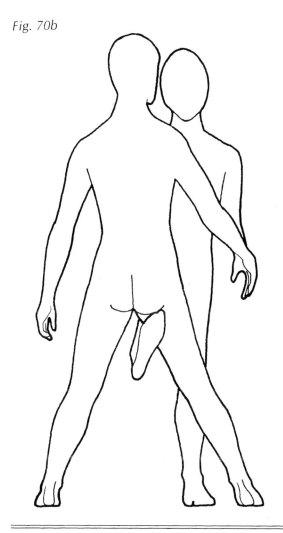

Fig. 70b

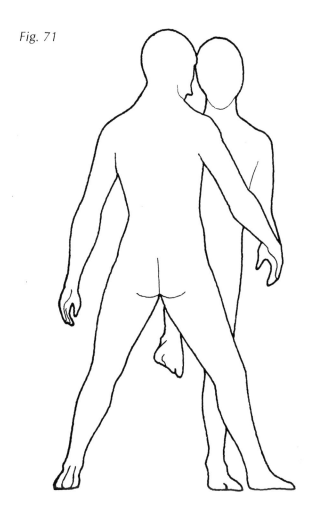

Fig. 71

Standing Noncontact Groin Kick

This illusion is identical to Standing Contact Groin Kick 1 except that the attacker's right foot stops one inch from the victim's right thigh, and the attacker creates the knap by striking his or her own right or left thigh, depending upon audience positioning (see Figure 71).

Reclining Groin Kick 1

Should we kick a man when he's down? Only a particularly honorless person would do such a thing. But such characters appear onstage, and character consistency is an important consideration in choreographing stage fights.

The victim lies flat on his back with the right knee bent and the upper thigh raised off the floor to allow room for the attacker's foot. The victim's legs are far apart. This position may be accounted for by having the victim groggily "regain consciousness" and attempt to stand up.

The attacker steps between the victim's legs with the left foot and strikes the rear muscular portion of the victim's left thigh with the flat instep of the right foot (see Figure 72 a). Note the attacker's angle of approach.

The force of the kick is directed laterally to the thigh, but the victim must react as though the kick were centered directly in the groin (see Figure 72 b).

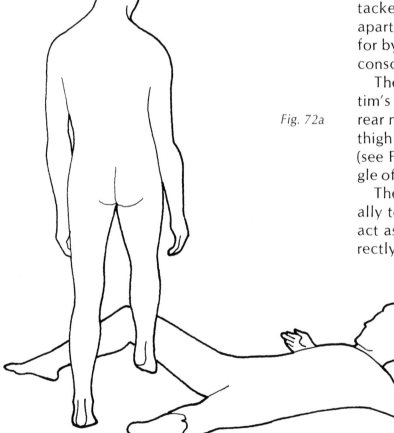

Fig. 72a

Reclining Groin Kick 2

This variation is a bit trickier than the first because the striking foot comes somewhat closer to the groin and coccyx. Practice slowly.

The victim lies flat on his back as in Reclining Groin Kick 1, except that in this variation the contracted buttocks are raised up off the floor with the legs bent and splayed (see Figure 73 a). The contracted buttocks are squeezed together to protect the lower spine and to prepare a buttock as a point of contact for the attacker's instep.

The attacker steps between the victim's legs, the supporting foot in alignment with the victim's centerline, and

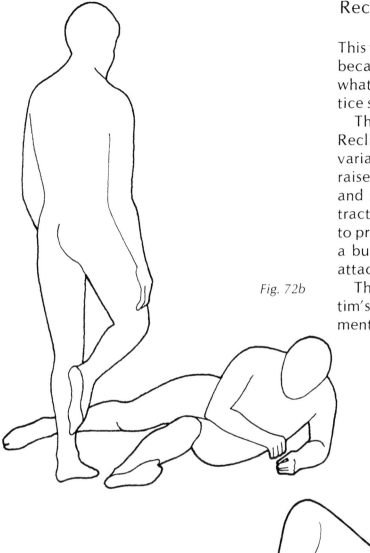

Fig. 72b

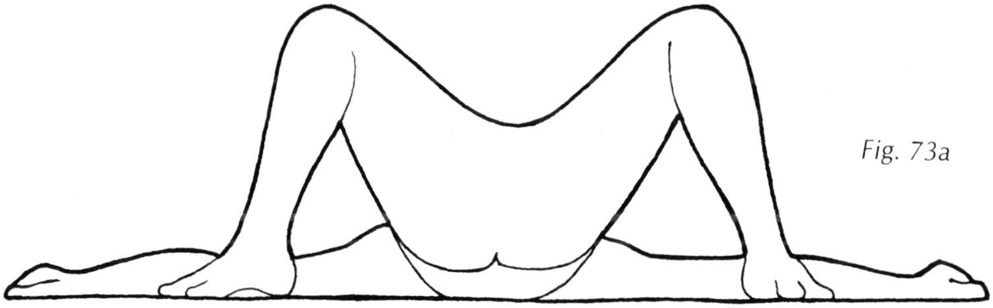

Fig. 73a

winds up by drawing the right leg back (see Figure 73 b). The attacker then swings the instep of the right foot forward, pivoting it primarily from the knee to diminish the leg's momentum. The attacker strikes the victim's left buttock and draws the foot back again to minimize the force (see Figure 73 c).

Slapping the thigh with the flat instep of the foot will create a believable sound with a minimum of force. The victim adds a vocal reaction following the knap and mimes the pain reaction to the groin kick.

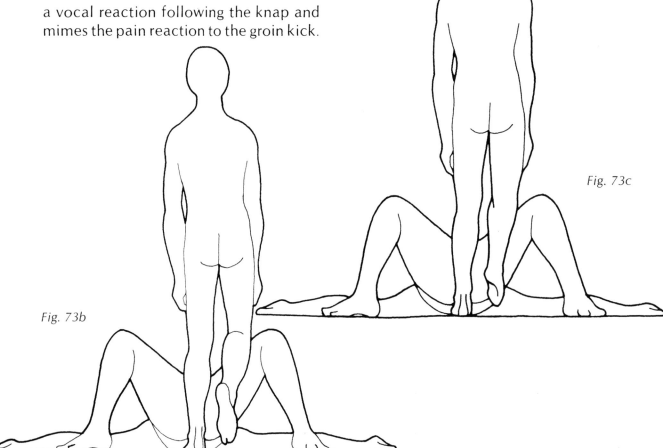

Fig. 73c

Fig. 73b

Rear-End Kick

This is usually a comic technique. Although I am outlining here a contact version, I've often seen clowns perform this illusion without contact at all, because their timing is perfect. This is one John Towsen, a nationally known authority on clowning and manager of *If Every Fool, Inc.,* would like.

The two important considerations in executing the Rear-End Kick are to avoid the base of the victim's spine and to minimize the force of impact.

If the attacker is kicking with the right foot, he or she stands to the left of the victim, slightly to the rear and facing the victim's left side (see Figure 74 a).

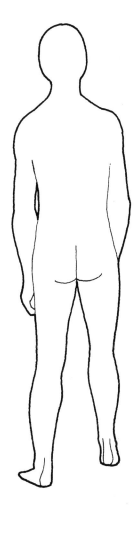

Fig. 74a

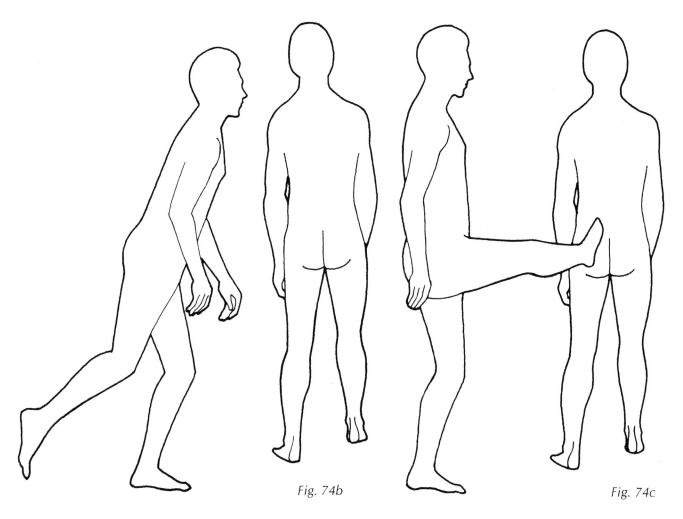

Fig. 74b

Fig. 74c

The attacker winds up and is aware of his or her own balance (see Figure 74 b). The attacker then kicks the victim's left buttock with the inside portion of the kicking foot, avoiding the victim's spine (see Figure 74 c). The kicking foot is pulled back immediately after making contact, in order to break its momentum and minimize the force.

The knap is created by the foot striking the buttock. Care must be taken not to kick too hard. And it is important never to kick the victim in the rear end with a pointed toe. To perform this technique while wearing large boots requires much practice.

Kick to the Shinbone

There are two essential points to remember when executing this simple and delightful technique. First, the sole of the foot is to be used to kick the lower leg (see Figure 75 a). For this reason, the attacker must have soft footwear. The kick occurs to one side of the shinbone, not on the shinbone itself (see Figure 75 b).

Second, the force of the kick must be minimized. The attacker must pull the foot back as soon as contact is made. Generally no knap is created from the contact between the attacker's foot and the victim's shinbone. However, vocal and physical reactions are sufficient theatrics.

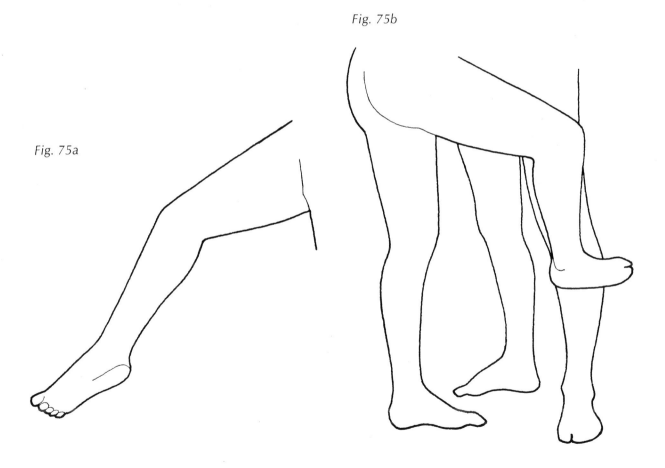

Fig. 75a

Fig. 75b

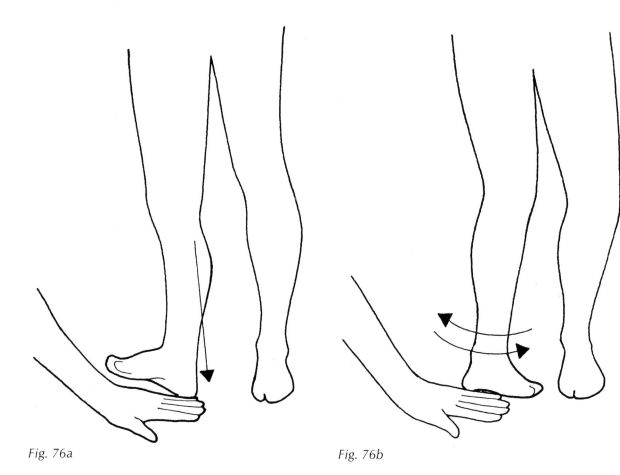

Fig. 76a

Fig. 76b

Stepping on a Hand

This is a purely mimed technique that depends on the pain reaction for dramatic impact.

The attacker puts a heel down on the floor to one side of the victim's hand, with the sole of the foot extending above the victim's hand. The foot is flexed, the toes pointing up toward the ceiling, leaving a space between the sole and the hand (see Figure 76 a).

To intensify the effect, the attacker can twist the foot from side to side, bending the knee to create the illusion of weight bearing down on the hand in a grinding movement (see Figure 76 b).

Stepping on the Head

This is another purely mimed technique, crucially dependent upon the attacker's ability to balance on one foot. This illusion is usually used for its comic effect in slapstick fights. You can try it with the victim lying prone, as shown, or kneeling with his or her head on the floor.

The victim lies prone on the floor with his or her head turned to face the attacker. The attacker places his left leg to one side of the victim's head (Figure 77a) and lowers the suspended (and flexed) right foot over the victim's head.

The victim grasps the attacker's ankle and foot and mimes pain and struggle — taking care not to upset the attacker's balance (see Figure 77 b). The attacker creates the illusion of bearing down upon the head by bending the knees of both legs.

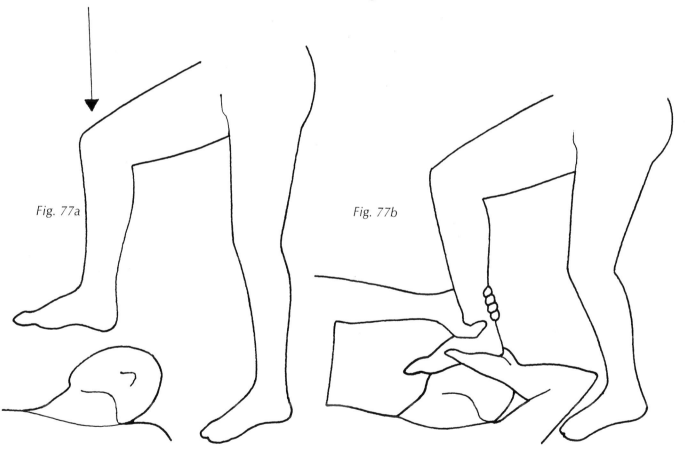

Fig. 77a

Fig. 77b

Foot Stomp

This is a classic slapstick technique used by old-time movie comics Stan Laurel and Oliver Hardy to begin a huge brawl. Use your imagination, as this illusion may be set up in any number of ways.

The victim presents the foot to be stepped upon. The attacker then lifts a flexed foot (Figure 78 a) and brings the heel down onto the floor next to the victim's foot (see Figure 78 b). The sole of the attacker's foot covers the victim's foot without actually touching it.

The sound of the attacker's heel striking the floor creates the knap. The victim adds vocal and physical pain reactions.

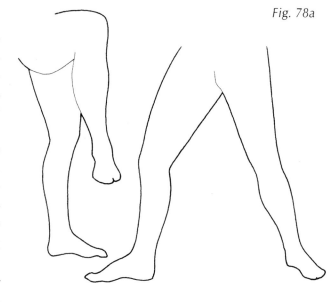

Fig. 78a

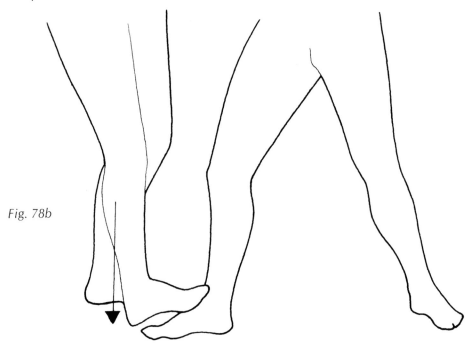

Fig. 78b

Stomping the Stomach

This illusion is a variation on the well-known all-star-wrestling technique of a knee drop to the back. Correct timing is essential to believability.

The victim lies down flat on his or her back with one or both knees up to aid abdominal contraction. The victim's contraction is only a safety measure, a precaution against accidents.

The attacker leaps into the air with the striking foot poised above the victim's stomach, presenting the flat sole of the foot to the stomach (see Figure 79 a).

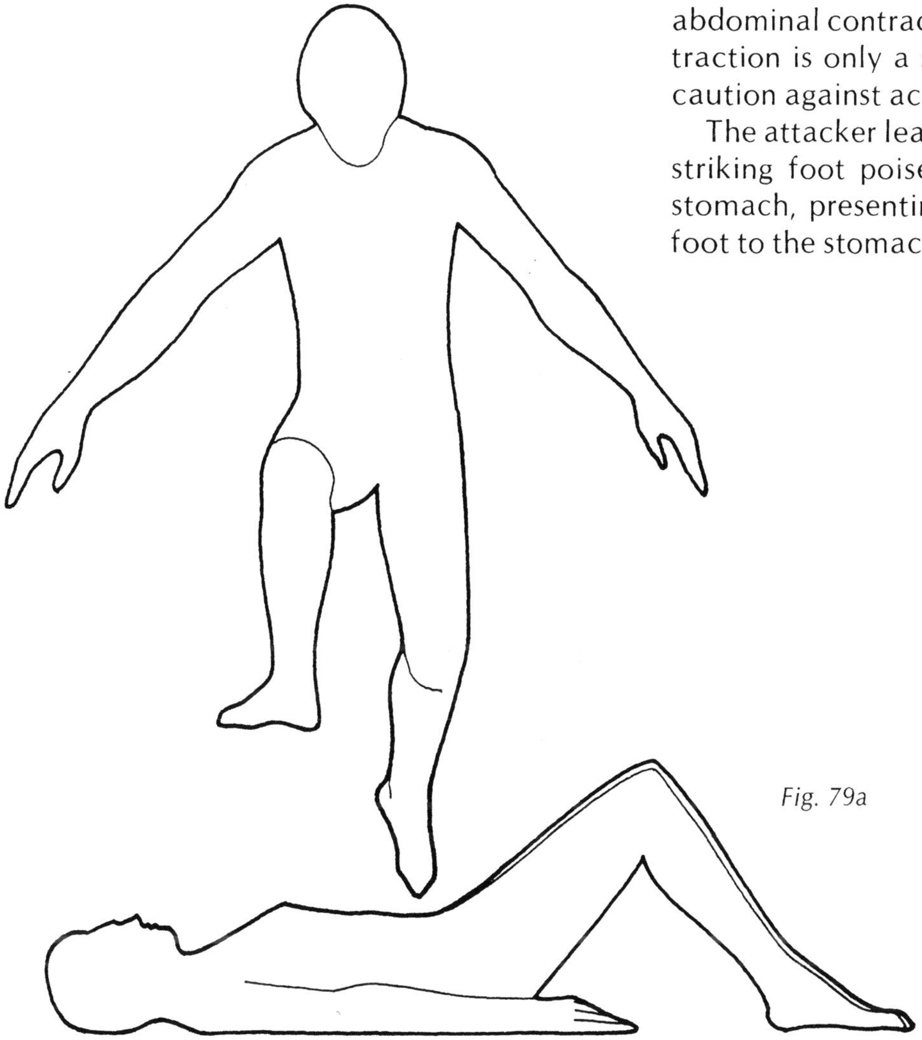

Fig. 79a

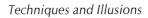

In a proscenium arch theatre, the attacker may be as much as six inches upstage of the victim, as long as the striking foot descends to a level that supports the illusion that the attacker's foot is striking the victim's stomach.

As the striking foot approaches to within about half an inch of the victim's contracted abdomen, the attacker's supporting foot strikes the floor very hard next to the victim, creating the knap (see Figure 79 b). The victim responds to the supposed blow to the stomach by curling up and adds a vocal grunt of pain.

The attacker can further support the illusion by withdrawing the "striking" foot just after the supporting foot creates the loud knap on the floor, creating the impression that the attacker's foot has rebounded from the victim's stomach.

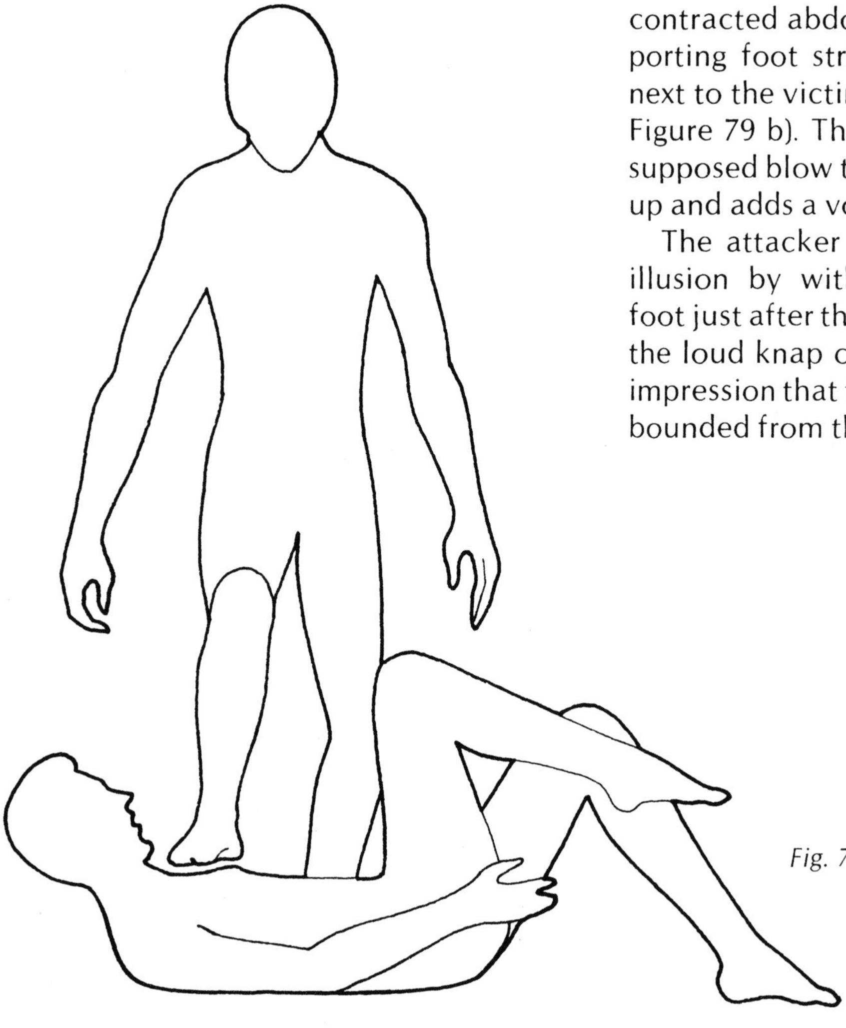

Fig. 79b

Knee Drop to the Back

This is a variation of a technique used by professional wrestlers, who often knee the back of a victim sprawled face down upon a wrestling mat. In this case the attacker must drop his own knee upon the mat to create the knap. On a hard stage surface, that variation is painful for the knees unless one uses knee pads.

This combat mime illusion is safer; it is very similar to Stomping the Stomach.

The victim is on his or her knees. The attacker is upstage of the victim and leaps into the air with the striking knee well bent (see Figure 80 a). How much the striking knee is bent during the leap is determined by the correct fighting distance in the position of supposed contact, as shown in Figure 80 b. The attacker's knee stops half an inch above the victim's back as the attacker's supporting foot strikes the floor, creating a knap.

The attacker's knee does not rebound, but instead remains bent as the attacker contracts all his or her muscles at the instant of supposed impact — i.e., when the supporting foot strikes the floor. The contraction creates the illusion that the attacker has struck something solid and fairly immovable.

Please remember that the knee drop and stomach stomp require a great deal of practice on the part of the attacker so that the striking foot or knee does not descend unto the victim's body by accident when the supporting foot hits the floor. The striking leg has a tendency to keep going after the other foot stops because gravity is forcing the leg's mass

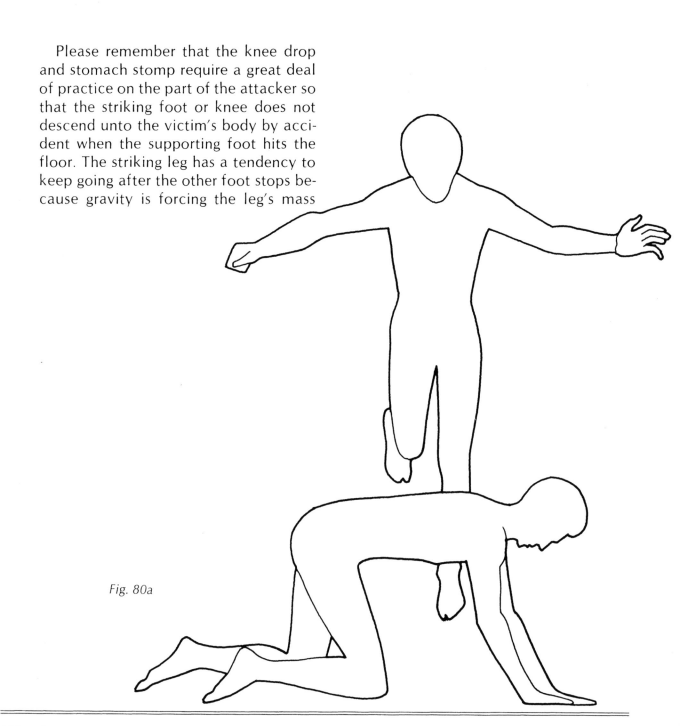

Fig. 80a

downwards. Practice using a low bench or stool in place of the victim until the leap and stop are completely mastered. Be sure the victim is the same height as the substitute!

Many beginning positions for the victim are possible. You'll find that the higher the victim's back is from the floor, the more difficult the illusion.

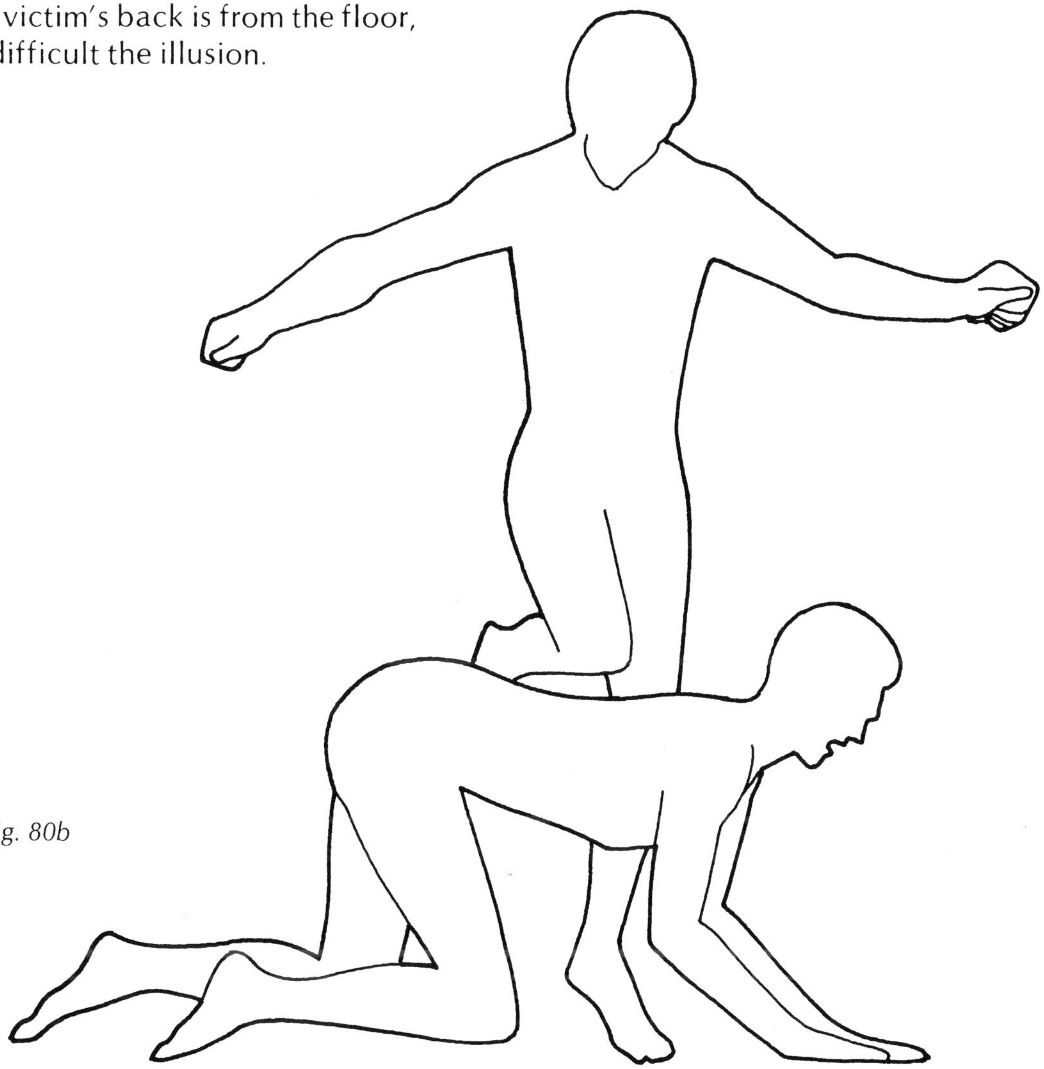

Fig. 80b

ASSORTED THROWS, SMASHES, DYING, LIFTING, AND DRAGGING

Here are a few more tricks to round out a fight. By now it should be quite clear that the creation of combat mime illusions is truly as limitless as your creative imagination! Strictly observe the elements of safety and then by all means improvise new techniques.

Overhead Foot Throw, to the Side

This is a simpler technique than the Overhead Foot Throw described below, but it creates a similar effect. You might want to use it as pretraining for the second version.

The attacker stands facing the victim, displaced to the victim's right side and with the right foot leading. The attacker grabs the victim's clothing at the upper chest with both hands (see Figure 81 a).

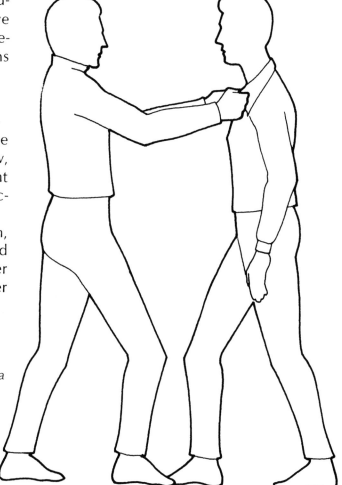

Fig. 81a

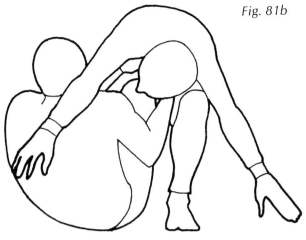

Fig. 81b

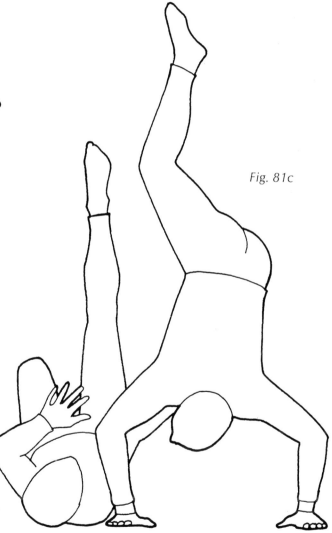

Fig. 81c

The attacker then bends the left leg and sits directly down on the floor, bringing the bent right knee up, while the victim steps forward with the left leg and prepares for a Dive Shoulder Roll by outstretching both arms and sighting a place beyond and to the right side of the attacker to begin the roll (see Figure 81 b).

The attacker sits and extends his or her arms backward in a follow-through. The attacker can also extend his or her right leg at the knee, creating the illusion of having kicked the victim overhead, as the victim performs a Dive Shoulder Roll and Layout. The roll and layout are actually performed completely clear of the attacker and to the attacker's right side (see Figure 81 c).

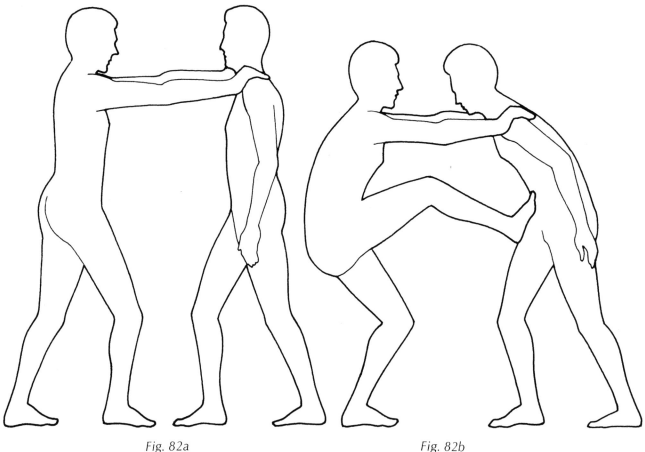

Fig. 82a

Fig. 82b

Overhead Foot Throw

You must have a well-established Dive Shoulder Roll, or forward Shoulder Roll and Layout to execute this technique most effectively.

The attacker stands directly in front of the victim, with his or her hands on the victim's shoulders (see Figure 82 a). The attacker bends the left leg, as though to sit back on the floor, and simultaneously places the right foot on the victim's stomach (see Figure 82 b). The attacker sits down, gliding to the floor, firmly holding on to the victim's shoulders. The victim, meanwhile, steps forward to the outside of the attacker's body with the intention of doing a forward roll beyond the attacker's head (see Figure 82 c).

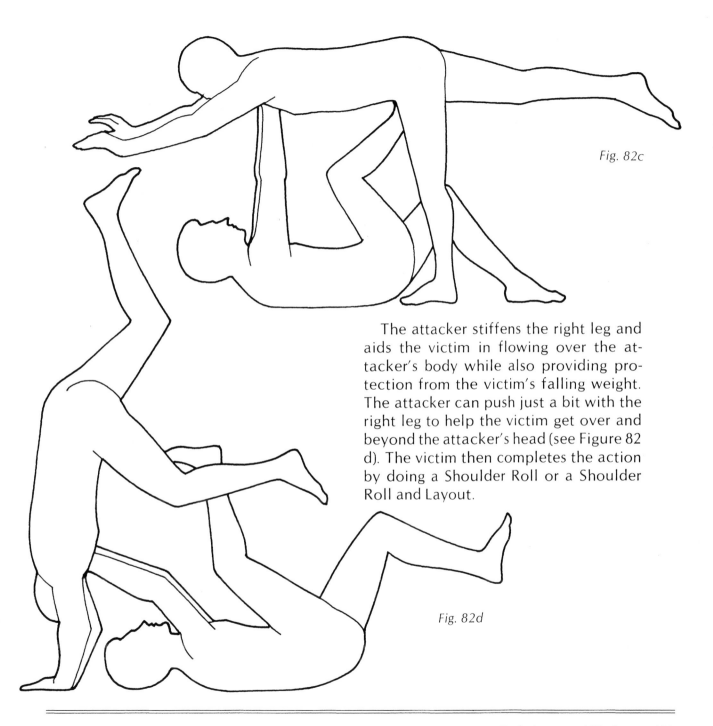

Fig. 82c

The attacker stiffens the right leg and aids the victim in flowing over the attacker's body while also providing protection from the victim's falling weight. The attacker can push just a bit with the right leg to help the victim get over and beyond the attacker's head (see Figure 82 d). The victim then completes the action by doing a Shoulder Roll or a Shoulder Roll and Layout.

Fig. 82d

Hip Throw

A delightful surprise can be created when a woman performs this technique on a man!

The attacker faces the victim and grasps the victim's right hand with his or

Fig. 83a

Fig. 83b

her own left hand. The attacker then steps in and past the victim's right foot, while placing the right arm beneath the victim's left arm. The attacker then places his or her right hip beneath the victim's right hip (see Figure 83 a). By twisting the hips to the left, the attacker can lift and throw the victim to the left, as shown in Figure 83 b.

The attacker can quite easily control the victim's descent by firmly holding the victim's body with the right arm and bending at the knees while lowering the victim's body to the floor (see Figure 83 c). The attacker should be very careful, when lowering the victim, to use the strength of the legs by fully bending the knees, not by bending from the waist — which may cause undo stress on the small of the back.

The victim should slap the floor with the left hand to cause the sound of impact with the floor, as shown by the arrow in Figure 83d.

Fig. 83c

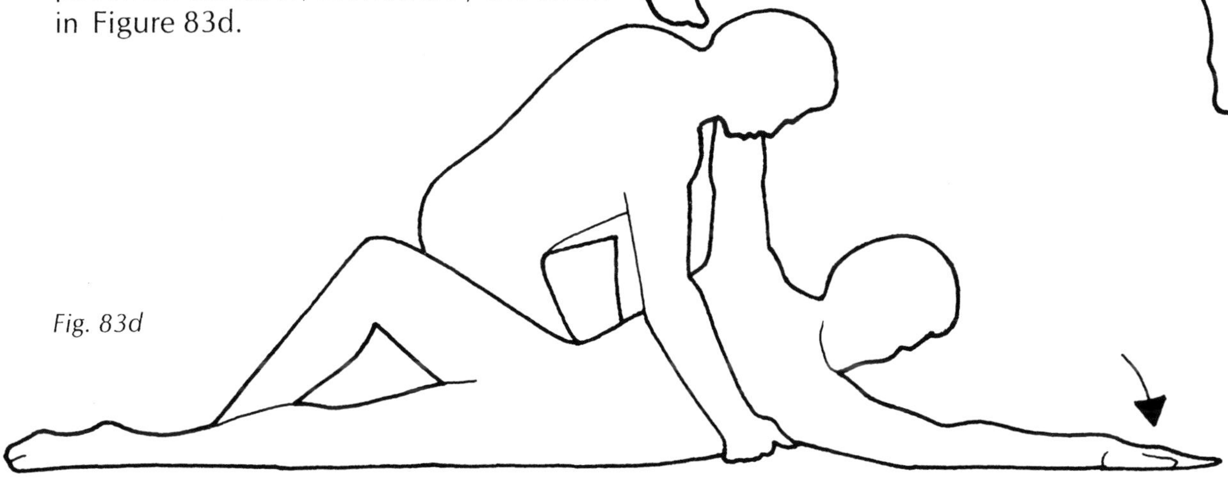

Fig. 83d

Head Throw

This technique is a wonderful example of the simple effectiveness of combat mime.

The attacker places his or her right hand on the back of the victim's head (see Figure 84 a). The victim performs a Dive Shoulder Roll and Layout, leading from the head to support the illusion of being thrown by the attacker. The attacker follows the victim's action toward the floor (see Figure 84 b).

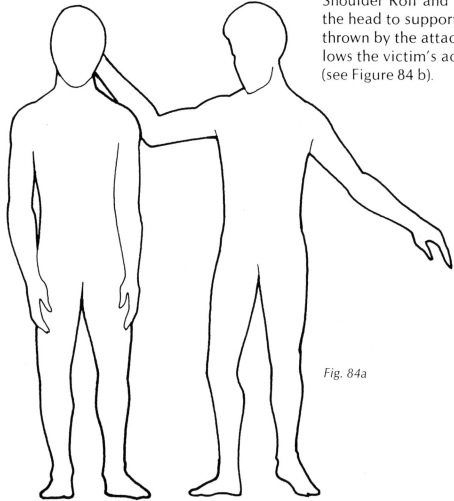

Fig. 84a

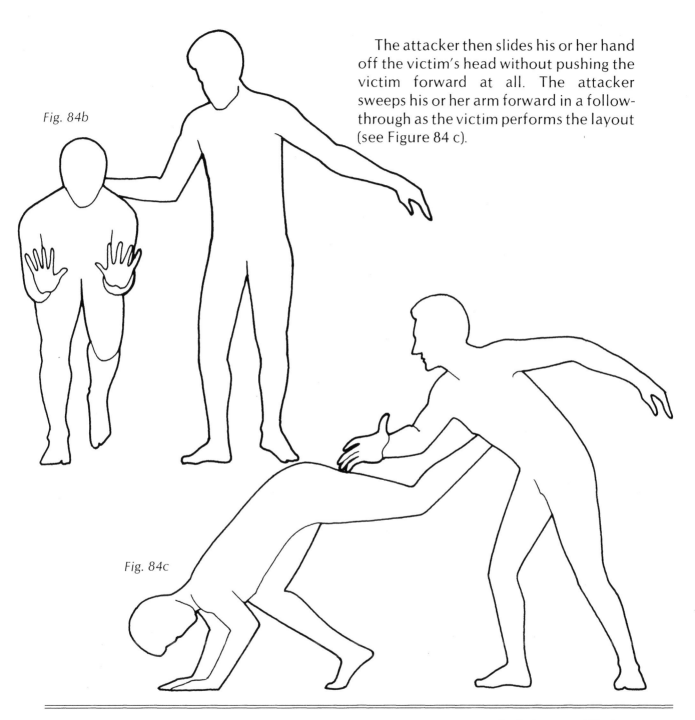

Fig. 84b

The attacker then slides his or her hand off the victim's head without pushing the victim forward at all. The attacker sweeps his or her arm forward in a follow-through as the victim performs the layout (see Figure 84 c).

Fig. 84c

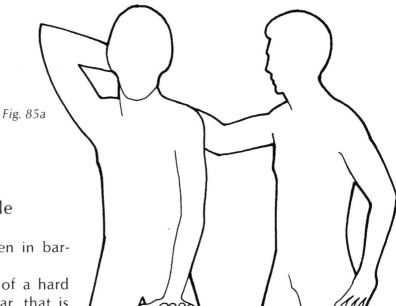

Fig. 85a

Head Smash against a Table

This technique is often seen in bar-room brawls.

The victim stands in front of a hard surface, such as a table or bar, that is roughly waist high. The victim's left hand is on the surface of the table and in alignment with the head. The victim's right hand is on top of the attacker's right hand, which is on the back of the victim's head. The attacker is standing to the victim's left (see Figure 85 a).

The illusion to strive for here is that the attacker is attempting to force the victim's head down onto the table as the victim resists. Mime this resistance for a few moments until the victim brings the head up slightly, then quickly brings it down, always looking at the table, and halts it about two inches above the left hand placed on the table. This hand will act as a cushion in case of a miscalculation (see Figure 85 b).

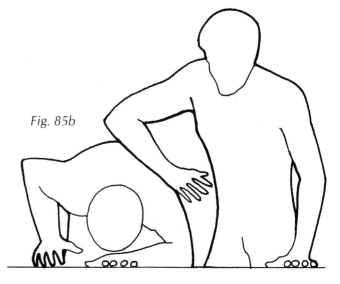

Fig. 85b

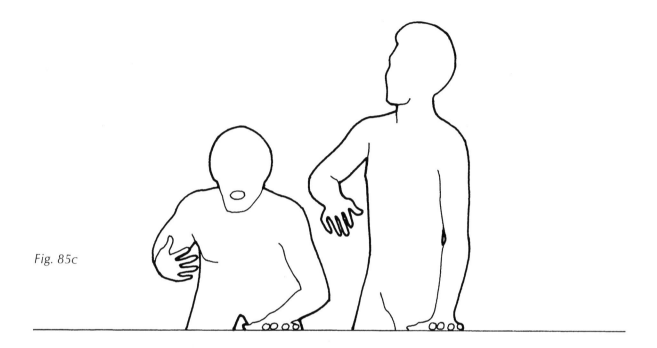

Fig. 85c

At the bottom of the victim's downward head swing (two inches away from the table), the victim strikes the surface of the table with the right hand to create the sound of impact and immediately allows the head to rebound from the table; these actions reinforce the illusion that the head has bounced against the hard surface with great force (see Figure 85 c).

Please remember to make eye contact just before the victim brings the head down toward the table. The attacker must not push at all on the back of the victim's head. And the victim must keep his or her eyes open as the head approaches the table, so as to avoid a collision. The victim must resist the instinctual urge to close the eyes.

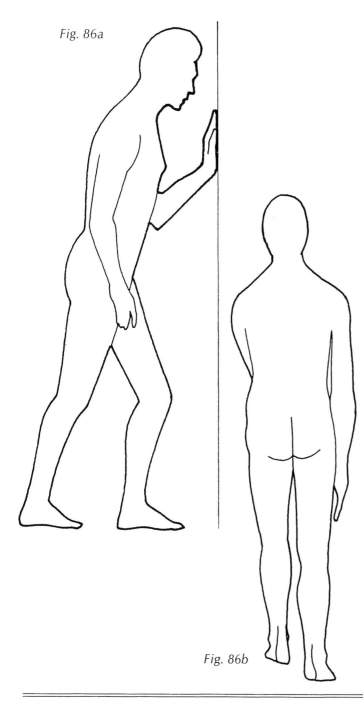

Fig. 86a

Fig. 86b

Head Smash against a Wall

Smashing the head against a wall is usually performed with a running start; therefore we must be especially concerned with controlling the momentum of the body hurtling towards the wall. Controlling the impact is the most important part of the technique and must be mastered before adding the actions of the attacker.

We will use the muscles of the victim's left thigh and upper left arm to act as a powerful spring to absorb the forward momentum, although if you feel more comfortable using the right thigh and arm, feel free to do so.

The victim begins by standing about six inches away from the wall, judging the distance from the toe of the leading left foot. The left hand should be against the wall (Figure 86 a); the elbow will be tucked in so that the audience will be unable to see the left arm and hand when viewing the action from downstage of the victim's back (see Figure 86 b).

The victim, beginning with the left foot, takes three steps away from the wall. From this distance the victim practices moving toward the wall and using the left leg and arm to cushion the impact with the wall.

I think it's important here to emphasize that the left thigh muscles are doing the vast majority of the work in protecting the body from hitting the wall. In fact,

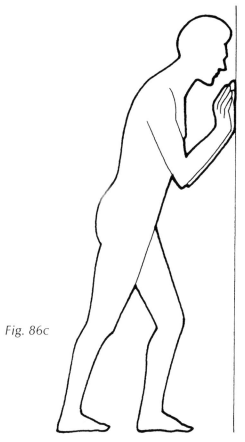

Fig. 86c

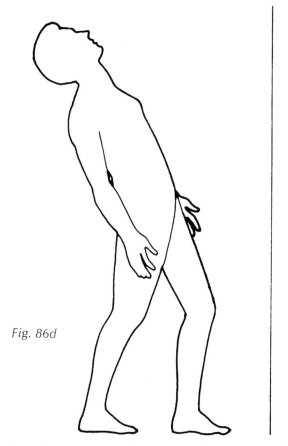

Fig. 86d

the victim can practice stopping without using the left hand just to reinforce the braking action of the left leg. The left arm is only a backup for the left leg.

After having practiced moving toward the wall from three steps away, the victim begins to increase the distance from the wall and up the running speed as well. Remember that combat mime illusions lose their effectiveness when not under absolute control.

The victim now practices adding the head reaction and creating the sound of impact. When the victim's head is about four inches away from the wall (the head leads, as this is a head smashing technique), the victim slaps the wall in front of the body with the right hand. The right elbow is tucked in (see Figure 86 c). The victim's head snaps back at the same time that the right hand strikes the wall, creating the illusion of impact. The weight of the victim's body then follows the direction of the rebounding head (Figure 86 d).

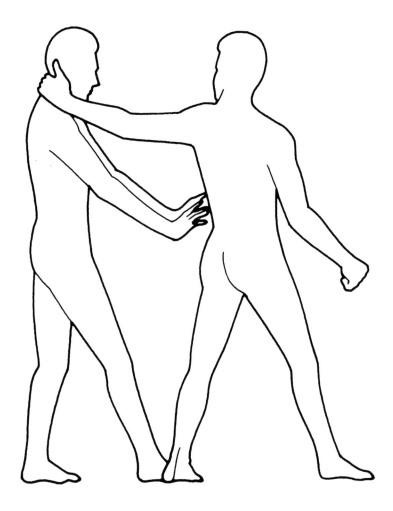

It may help the victim to note that the focus is not on hitting the wall but on rebounding from it. Think *away* from the wall as soon as you touch it with the springing left hand.

The attacker now begins to practice with the victim by standing on the victim's right side, placing his or her left hand on the back of the victim's neck (the attacker could use the hair pulling technique). The attacker merely follows the victim's lead. However, please note that the attacker does remain slightly in advance of the victim to create the illusion of pulling the victim toward the wall (see Figure 86 e).

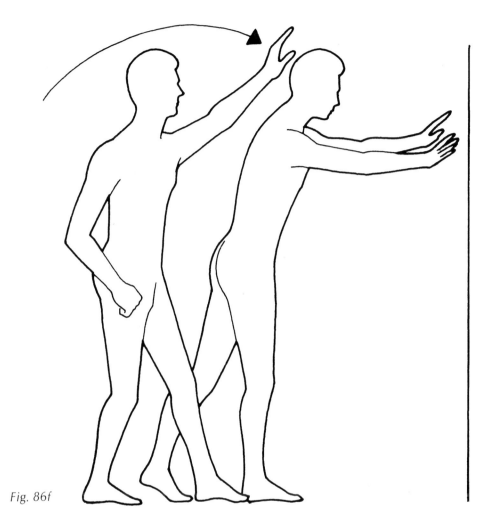

Fig. 86f

When the victim is about two feet from the wall, the attacker slides his or her left hand straight up, clearing the victim's head, and follows through with a sweeping arc of the left arm across the body, as though propelling the victim the last few feet toward the wall (see Figure 86 f). This not only creates a powerful illusion of speed and force, but frees up the victim entirely to deal with control techniques and reactions.

Head Smash against the Floor

Fig. 87a

As I will mention again when dealing with choreography, always suit the action to the situation. A technique like this is appropriate only in particularly vicious fights, on the one hand, or candidly slapstick routines on the other.

The victim lies on his or her stomach with the left hand outstretched directly beneath the head, to act as a cushioning safeguard. The right arm is tucked in close to the body with the right hand flat to the floor below the upper chest (see Figure 87 a).

The attacker straddles the victim and places his or her hands on the victim's head (see Figure 87 b). The victim, taking a cue from the physical contact of the attacker's hands, lifts the head straight up and back as though being pulled up by the attacker (see Figure 87 c). Next, the victim brings the head sharply down toward the floor, keeping the eyes open and stopping an inch or two short of the floor. At the supposed moment of impact, the victim slaps the floor with the right hand, pivoting from the wrist.

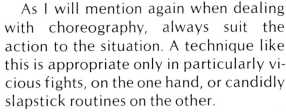

Fig. 87b

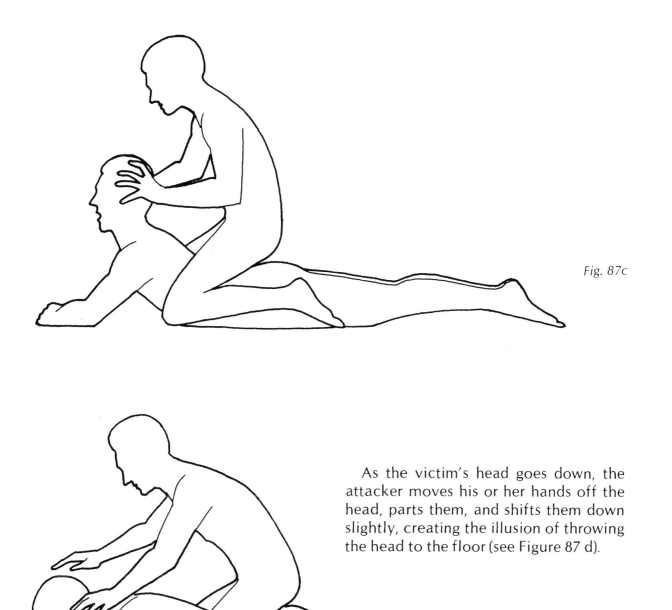

Fig. 87c

As the victim's head goes down, the attacker moves his or her hands off the head, parts them, and shifts them down slightly, creating the illusion of throwing the head to the floor (see Figure 87 d).

Fig. 87d

The victim jerks the head slightly up as though the skull were rebounding from the floor (Figure 87 e). The victim's reaction should ripple through the body and into the legs as well.

The attacker must have a very light touch on the victim's head, never pushing or pulling. The attacker must be able to sense the victim's intentions. Practice will perfect the timing. And victim, please remember to keep your eyes open when approaching the floor.

This technique is most effective if repeated more than once.

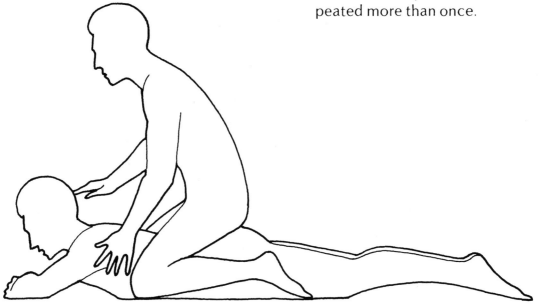

Fig. 87e

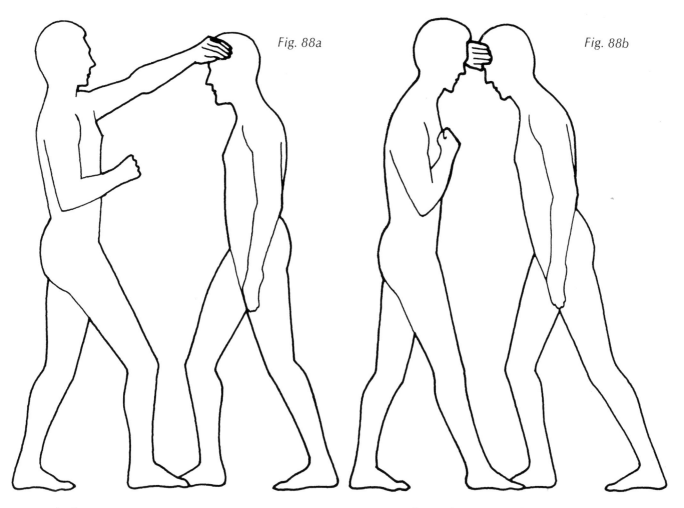

Fig. 88a

Fig. 88b

Head Butt

The attacker stands directly in front of the victim and places the left palm high on the victim's forehead. The hand on the forehead acts as a safeguard against accidental contact and establishes fighting distance at the same time (see Figure 88 a).

The victim and attacker *maintain eye* *contact throughout the illusion.* The attacker pulls the head back slightly in a windup, then whips it toward the victim and stops the forward momentum when the partners' eyes are approximately two inches away (see Figure 88 b). At that moment the attacker strikes his or her own chest squarely in the center with a closed fist to create the hollow crack of the Head Butt.

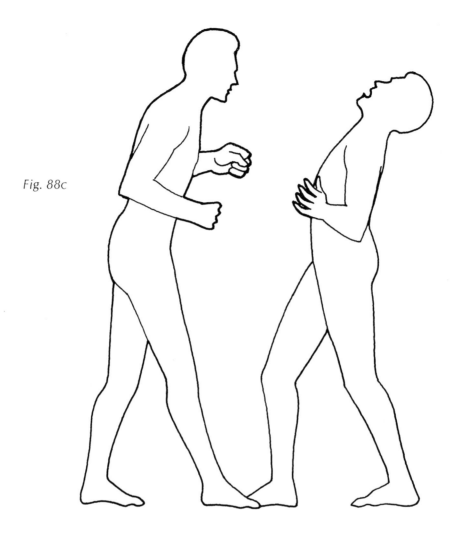

Fig. 88c

The victim then reacts backwards, allowing the head to recoil first with the weight of the body following (see Figure 88 c).

The attacker must not use the hand on the victim's forehead to push the victim backwards, either to help the action or through an involuntary response.

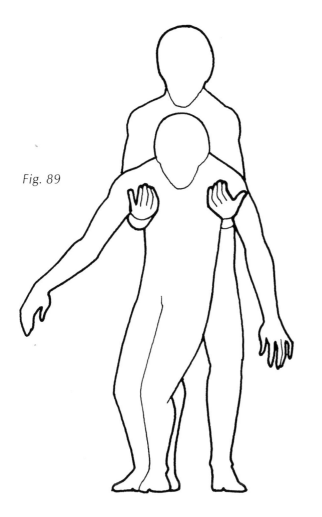

Fig. 89

Fainting

Many of you have seen someone faint in films, television, or in real life; perhaps you have noticed that the fainting body follows the laws of gravity as it falls. It makes a fairly gentle descent.

Use the Side Fall technique outlined earlier when performing a Faint.

If someone is to catch the fainting victim before he or she hits the ground, the victim must extend the arms out to the sides at the beginning of the fall. The catcher will then grab the victim from behind, using the victim's armpits as points of contact (see Figure 89).

Dying

All I wish to say concerning this subject involves common sense. Remember to focus on the area of pain — knife thrust in chest, axe in back, poison in belly, etc. — and as Shakespeare so eloquently warned: "Suit the action to the word, the word to the action; with this special observance, that you o'erstep not the modesty of nature."

One more note: the key to "dying" effectively on stage lies in the altering of the victim's breathing rhythms.

Lifting and Carrying a Body

Here are two techniques designed to save the muscles of the lower back. The first method does connote some concern, or respect for the body, while the second suggests disregard.

The Cradle

The victim is lying outstretched on his or her back.

The lifter crouches down on one knee and lifts the nearest arm, appearing to cause the victim to sit up; however, the victim is actually doing the sitting up, using the stomach muscles, while keeping the arms and head limp. The lifter places the victim's arm behind his or her neck (see Figure 90 a).

The victim must now surreptitiously stiffen the arm around the attacker's neck, keeping the hand limp, as this will aid greatly in the lift. The lifter then slides an arm underneath both of the victim's knees, as the victim brings the knees up with the feet still dragging on the floor (see Figure 90 b). Although the victim is

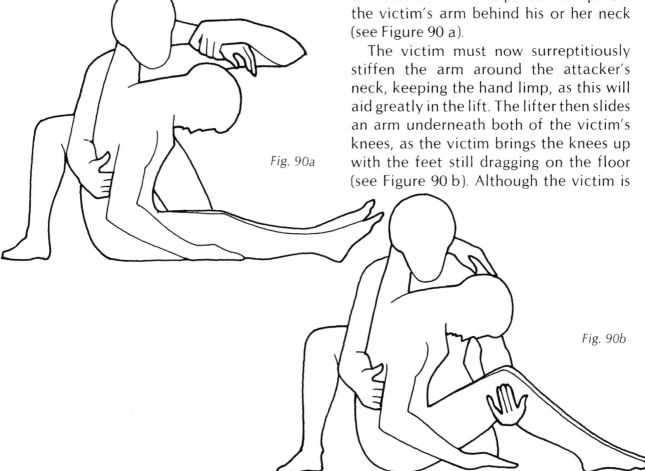

Fig. 90a

Fig. 90b

doing the work of lifting the legs, the audience must not know it.

Next, the lifter shifts the victim's body onto his or her own knee. The lifter must be close to the victim to accomplish this (see Figure 90 c).

Using the muscles of the thigh, not bending from the waist, the lifter lifts and cradles the victim's body (see Figure 90 d). The victim should stiffen the body but keep the head, neck, feet, and hands limp and relaxed.

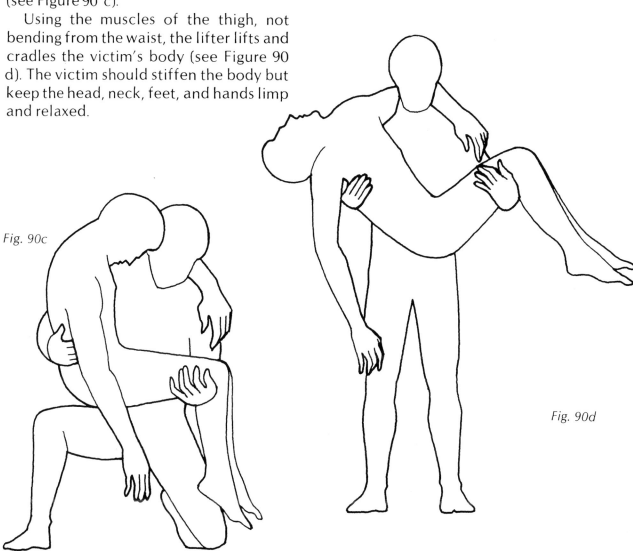

Fig. 90c

Fig. 90d

Fireman's Carry

The victim must be lying in a prone position. The lifter picks up both of the victim's arms and places his or her right foot at the base of the victim's feet, so that the victim does not slide during the lift. Stepping back on the left foot to shift his or her own weight, the lifter pulls on the victim's arms. At the same time, the victim stiffens his or her bent knees and pivots upright (see Figure 91a).

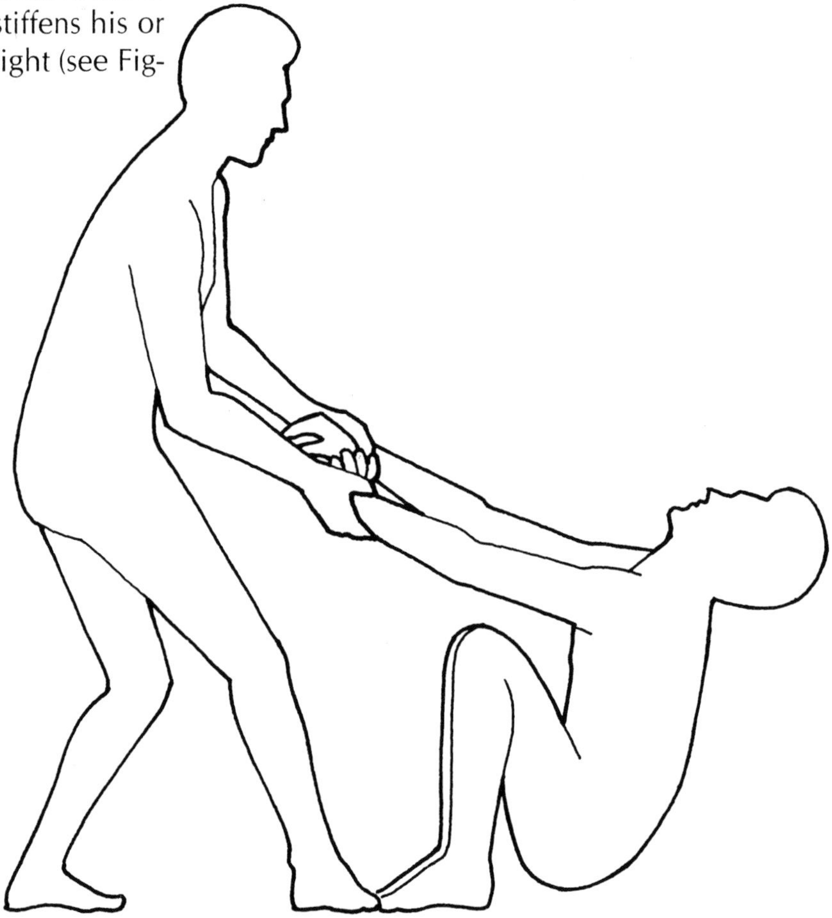

Fig. 91a

The lifter bends in the knees and moves forward to allow the victim's body to fall over from the waist onto the lifter's right shoulder (see Figure 91 b). The lifter straightens the knees in time to utilize the victim's falling weight for a smooth lift (see Figure 91 c).

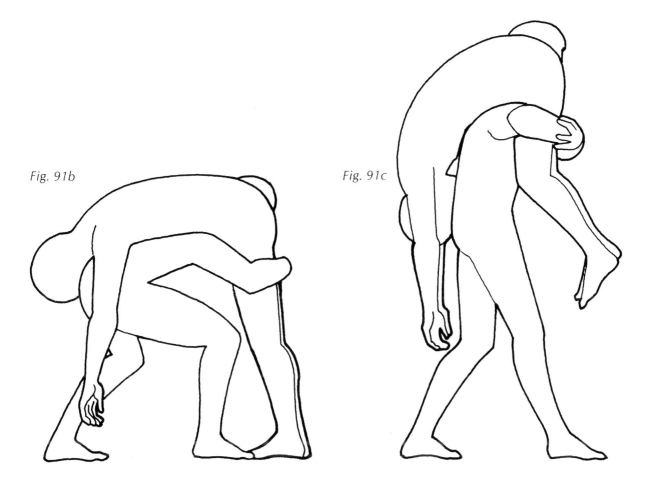

Fig. 91b

Fig. 91c

Underarm Drag

The only trick in this technique is that the victim secretly tightens the muscles of the shoulders and chest to aid the lifter.

Initially the victim is lying down. The lifter approaches the victim's head end, crouches down, and grasps the victim's underarms (see Figure 92 a). By using the muscles of the thighs and keeping the back flat, the lifter straightens his or her

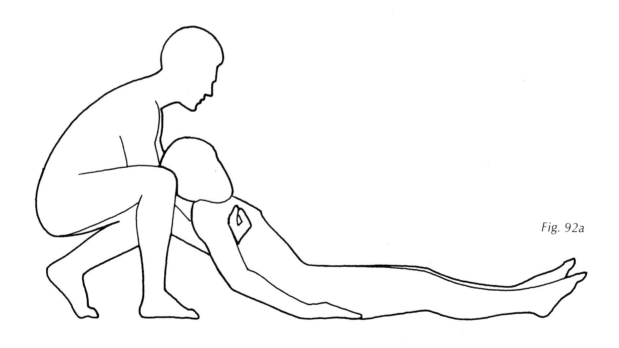

Fig. 92a

knees, lifting the victim's upper body clear of the floor (see Figure 92 b). The victim, meanwhile, is tightening the muscles of his or her chest and shoulders while keeping the head, arms, and legs limp, so as to give the attacker a firm grip beneath the arms.

The victim is lifted high enough to avoid either hitting the victim's head with the attacker's knees or forcing the attacker to bend forward from the waist.

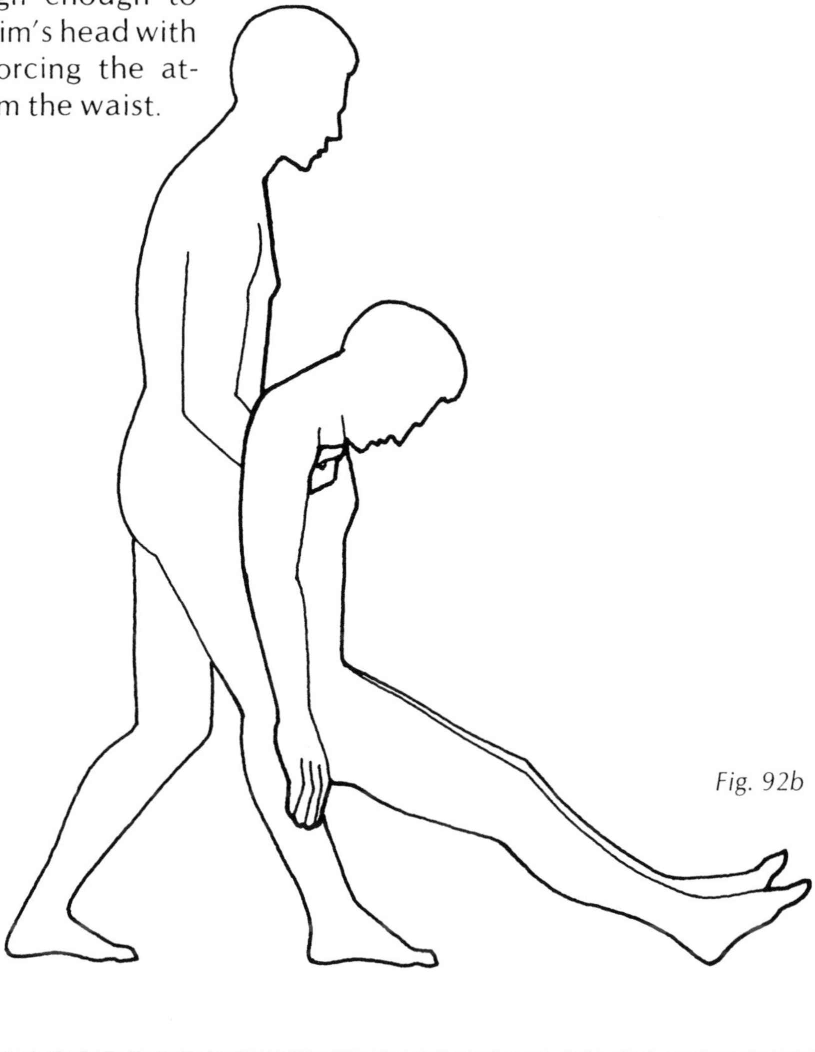

Fig. 92b

One-Wrist Drag

A strong soldier can quickly clear a stage two victims at a time by dragging each by a wrist.

If the victim is lying flat on his or her back, the head must be raised very slightly off the floor during the drag (see Figure 93 a). It is sometimes helpful if the victim also tightens the abdominal muscles, thus raising the buttocks off the floor, so that only the heels and lower legs drag on the floor.

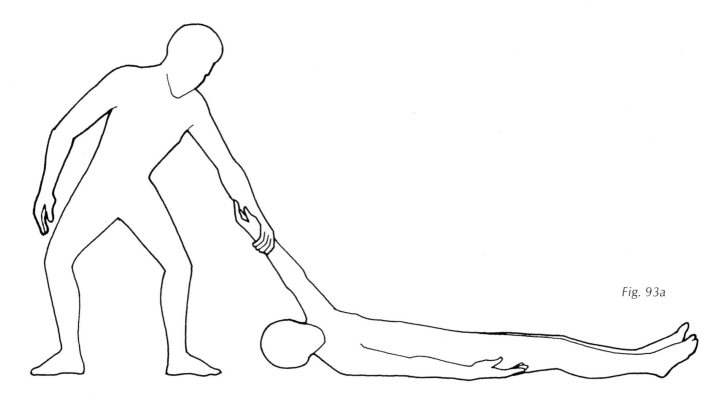

Fig. 93a

If the victim is face down on the floor, the attacker should drag the victim so that the extended arm is "beneath" the victim's head (see Figure 93 b).

Please note that the victim's "limp" hand is dragging along the floor, actually acting as a guide to prevent the victim's body from twisting. The victim's legs are slightly apart to resist twisting during the drag.

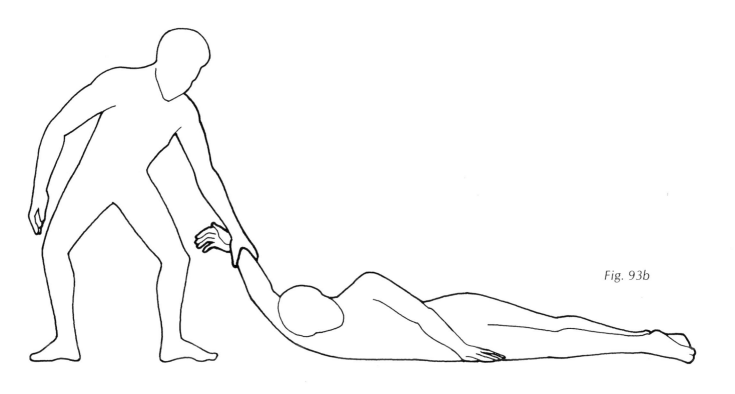

Fig. 93b

Two-Wrist Drag

This technique begins with the victim lying on his or her back. The attacker drags the victim by both wrists, taking care to lift the victim's head clear of the floor (see Figure 94 a). The attacker must take very small steps so as not to accidentally kick the victim's head.

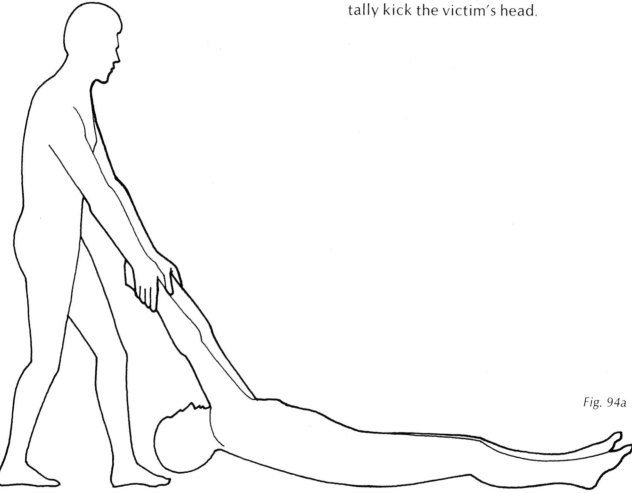

Fig. 94a

The attacker may find this technique easier if he or she twists the hips and lower legs in the direction of drag (see Figure 94 b).

Clear the stage floor of nails, staples, etc., and watch out for splinters on a wooden floor!

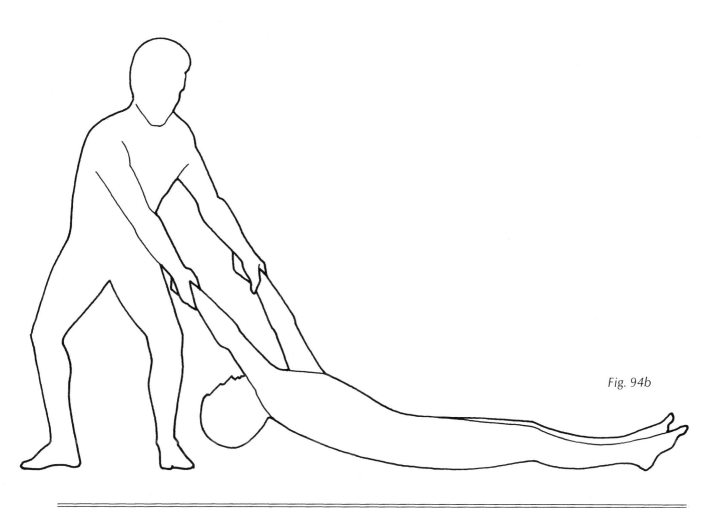

Fig. 94b

Choreography

Many spokes unite to form the wheel but it is the center that makes it useful.

Fights cannot be choreographed from reading a book. In fact, it's a dangerous undertaking to attempt to choreograph a fight from merely reading this, or any other, book. Direct experience is the best form of learning, and the safest way to learn how to choreograph stage fights is to hire a professional fight choreographer (certified by the Society of American Fight Directors) and observe his or her work. For, although a picture is worth a thousand words, an experienced choreographer is worth a thousand pictures. Having said that, what I would like to share with you in this chapter are suggestions and helpful hints I have gleaned from the ten years or so that I've been involved in stage fight choreography.

The theatre is a collective art form, perhaps more so than any of the other arts. We who practice the theatre arts are by necessity ruled by creative compromise. The final production must be an integration of all the elements of the art of the theatre, and the fight choreographer must acknowledge all the elements of the production and be able to work creatively with all the members of the production team. The fight choreographer is a specialist among a team of specialists, where the sum is greater than its individual parts.

WORKING WITH THE DIRECTOR

The director's responsibility encompasses the entire production, and he or she must have final say on all aspects of the production, creative and otherwise. It's important for the fight choreographer to ask the director a few essential questions before beginning any conceptualization of the proposed fights. (Of course the fight choreographer has long since read the play and is thoroughly familiar with it.)

1. How many fights will there be in the production?
2. How many actors will be in each fight?
3. What is the director's conception of the characters and what, if any, special idiosyncratic tendencies do they have? What would the director like to see revealed about the individual characters during the fight?
4. What does the director hope to convey to the audience dramatically within the fight?
5. What special effects does the director envisage?

6. How much rehearsal time is available for fight choreography?
7. What is the overall rehearsal schedule?
8. When can the fighters expect to be able to rehearse on stage? On set?
9. Is there to be music with the fights? Who will choose the music?
10. When are the preproduction meetings planned?
11. What are the names and phone numbers of the production team?
12. If fights are important to the show will the director want the fight choreographer to help conduct auditions?

WORKING WITH THE STAGE MANAGER

The stage manager (SM) is a very important person for the fight choreographer because, long after the fight choreographer has gone his merry way, the SM must faithfully see to it that the actors do their prescribed combat warm-up prior to each show, as well as keep a wary eye on the integrity of the fight choreography over the run of the show. A very important person indeed! Sometimes the assistant stage manager will assume these duties.

I insist that the SM consistently attend

all the technique practices and the choreography rehearsals so as to be more attuned to the needs and concerns of the actors involved in the fights.

All of the notated fight choreography is given to the SM for inclusion in the prompt book, in case altercations arise among combatants during the run of the show.

The SM is also taught the preshow warm-up, so that he or she can conduct it from time to time to reinforce its professional seriousness to the combatants. In most cases, however, the combatants are well aware of the importance of a preperformance warm-up. During the warm-up, the combatants will walk through their fights and the SM will refer to the written choreography in the prompt book to check for discrepancies. Therefore it is important that the choreographer methodically outline the choreographed fights with the SM so that the latter is thoroughly familiar with notated fights. Usually this process will occur spontaneously during rehearsals; however do not be adverse to taking a separate rehearsal just to solidify the SM's understanding of the fights in detail. In the remote eventuality of an injury's occurring onstage during a fight, it will be the SM's responsibility to stop the fight; therefore it is essential that the he or she be very familiar with the fight as it is usually performed. Sometimes an injured actor gets caught up in the "show must go on" syndrome, insists that the injury is minor, and wants to continue, but of course an injured performer must never be allowed to continue a stage fight.

WORKING WITH ACTORS

Actors are people. They have both abilities and limitations. The fight choreographer must know the actors' qualities as combatants very intimately and very quickly, if the fight is to be truly safe and effective. For example, it is a waste of time to insist that an actor leap off a ten-foot tower during a fight if that actor is afraid of heights! Or why give a combatant who can't wear contact lenses and is virtually blind without glasses a large number of key exchanges in a group fight? Of course one hopes that intelligent casting will prevent such problems, but all too often the demands of the stage fights are not thoroughly considered when casting is done (another argument for including the fight choreographer in the audition process).

As I have stated earlier in this book, if the fight choreographer is thorough and methodical in training the actors, they will feel more comfortable and less likely to go hog wild in a performance or become fearful and inaccurate and unwilling to try new things in rehearsal. Actors are for the most part eager and resourceful individuals who will often surprise you if given a little honest respect and gentle encouragement.

Don't overload your actors with too much detail too soon in the rehearsal process. They will naturally make mistakes in balance, style, dynamic, etc., but be patient. Give your actors time to assimilate the choreography. If you give them too much too soon, they have a much harder time memorizing the fight in the long run. Remember the body learns in a different way than the mind. Give the body the time to feel the choreography through simple repetition of short sections of the fight before moving on to new information.

Be definite in your direction. It is best to have the combatants learn a sequence before changing it. There will be time to change things once the basic fight is learned. It's much easier for actors to add new bits than it is for them to change or cut out sections of the fight while they are learning it.

Have a cutoff date for changes. Past a certain rehearsal do not change any choreography, but concentrate on solidifying and improving the fight so that the combatants are very confident to perform in public. My rule of thumb with skilled performers is to stop changing or adding new things to the fight at least three rehearsal periods before first dress rehearsal.

WORKING WITH DESIGNERS

Theatre training schools in the United States are becoming increasingly aware of the importance of the fight choreographer within the theatre arts. However, at the present time designers largely ignore the basic design needs of the fight choreographer. For example, some costume designers never think of talking to the fight choreographer, even when designing *Romeo and Juliet;* set designers overlook essential padding on a staircase or even the proper width of a stair tread, even though a choreographer will be teaching an actor how to fall down the stairs. I've encountered a choreographer who complained that he'd rehearsed and practiced his fights in full light for three weeks; yet at the first technical rehearsal he'd discovered that the stage was almost in total darkness! Actually, in a case like this the choreographer shares the blame – communication, early communication, is the key.

Prior to any designs or renderings, definitely prior to any construction, the fight choreographer must be involved with the production team to assay the particular needs of the actor/combatants as the choreographer or the director sees them. Also, the fight choreographer must get an idea of what the designers are contemplating, so that he or she may more intelligently create the fights. A mutual appreciation of the roles of the designers and the fight choreographer, with the spirit of constructive and creative compromise, is the ticket! Be sure to be included in all the production meetings.

SETS

The concerns a choreographer may have over a set design are obvious. How much playing area is there? The confines of usable fighting space will determine the number of fighters who can be used or the way in which a choreographer creates flow patterns within a group fight. Are many levels or step units envisaged by the set designer? Is the stage surface to be padded or not? Raked? Are there to be many props, set pieces? Are furniture pieces practical or merely decorations? If a particular sofa, desk, table, or chair is to be used in a fight, is it built sturdily enough to take the use? Is there enough

clearance to land downstage out of a roll, or is there enough room between the piece of furniture and the flat? These details are best decided upon earlier rather than later. Often costs and time do not permit last-minute changes in the set to accommodate the creative urges of the fight choreographer.

Very definitely the quality of any fight will be affected by available stage space. During rehearsals it is essential to know how much room the fighters will have, in order to train properly and to test the feasibility of particular moves.

It is also very important to have platforms and step units constructed early in the rehearsal process, so that the combatants have an opportunity to work on the actual performance surfaces. Speaking of surfaces, some are definitely better than others. A slick linoleum or Masonite stage combined with a rake is treacherous; however, a plywood surface covered with half an inch of fiberboard and sized muslin is very nice for rolls and falls.

Of course, even before the designer sits down to the board to begin work, the director and choreographer must have a clear conception of special needs that may influence the overall design concept. For example, if the director wants a particularly heinous villain to fall ten feet while in flames, in a spectacular demise, it is essential that the set designer take into account the necessary masking for fire dousers, landing cushions, etc.

COSTUMES

Costumes are intimately linked with the conception and execution of any fight. The costume designer and the fight choreographer must make mutually advantageous decisions prior to any construction or choreography. All details of the costumes – hats, gloves, shoes, etc. – must be known before embarking on choreography or construction.

The qualities of period movement actually are largely dictated by the strictures of the dress of the period. Beyond historical considerations, however, we may need to mask special blood or broken bone effects through costuming.

Often an actor is called upon to do a particularly nasty fall, which requires the protection of padding at the elbows or knees. Sometimes it is necessary to pad an actor along the spine, or over the back of the shoulders or at the pelvis and hips. The costume designer must be aware of these needs so as to design the protective devices into the costume.

Footwear is an aspect of costume design that is very important to fight choreography. An actor/combatant needs posi-tive traction as well as a firm, tight fit to ensure balance and stability. Sometimes the choreographer must alter the conception and techniques of a particular fight because of costume design; after all, compromise is the name of the theatre game. For example, the costumer may require that the combatants wear large, heavy boots. This will mean that the choreographer must make special adjustments when choreographing kicking techniques, or perhaps eliminate kicking altogether in the fight.

Another costume concern that is often a point of conflict between the costume designer and the fight choreographer is the use of "blood." Should it be used at all? How will it affect the job of the costume crew? Will the blood be washable? Should any white or light-colored clothing be worn?

Stage blood is a useful tool if used sparingly; at times it is essential to the action as outlined by the playwright in the script. (I'll speak more about blood recipes and fabrics in the section on special effects.) If blood is going to be used, it must be seen; so if the blood is to get onto the costume during the course of a fight, then the fabric must be light enough to show the blood off to good advantage. However, it is not always necessary, when using blood, to get it on the costume. Nevertheless, accidents do happen, so it's best to plan for the occasional mishap by designing costumes for the eventuality that the blood will find its way onto the costume.

If a special effect such as a "broken arm" is to be used, then a sleeve to cover the effect is essential. If the choreographer wants the clothing to be ripped during a fight, this must be worked out well in advance with the designer!

MUSIC

As we all know from watching staged fights on television and film, music can be a most powerful asset to a dramatic or comic fight. The music can be used merely to underscore a fight by creating a mood or it can serve as a guide to orchestrating and choreographing the fight; in the same way that dances are choreographed to music. The advantages of choreographing a fight to music are that the fighters seem to learn the fight more thoroughly and safely that way, and the fight can be dramatically focused and underscored by the music. But choreography set to music is often more time consuming. If you have a limited amount of rehearsal time, then I recommend that the choreographer use music as a device to create an overall mood.

Setting a fight to music is best done with a metronome in the early stages of the rehearsal process, so that the combatants learn very technically the tempo-rhythms of the fight. Later, the fight, or sections of the fight, are repeated over and over with a recording of the music. If live music is to be used, then it is wise to have the musicians at several of the later rehearsals so they can work with the combatants, and the fight and music can become a unified experience.

When the fight has been successfully choreographed to the music, or even if music is only used as background effect, go over the fight with the sound technician so that the proper sound levels can be determined. If the only opportunity for doing this is at the first technical rehearsal of the entire show, have an understanding with the director and technical director that the time will be taken to set sound levels for the fight, so that the sounds of impact, or vocal reactions, will be heard.

LIGHTING

Stage lights are a powerful medium for defining space and creating mood. Of course the actors need enough light to see during the fight, but in addition, a stage fight's dramatic qualities can be greatly enhanced by using light to point up certain portions of a fight or areas of a stage. In group fights, it is sometimes effective to vary the lighting during the fight. For example, bright flashes of light may indicate offstage explosions, flickering light may convey a fire, or strobe lighting may pick up isolated tableaus during the fight. If the audience can see only select sections of a fight, they fill in the gaps from their own creative imaginations. Of course using only silhouettes to define a fight has long been effective in film and on the stage.

Naturally all choices must take into account whether or not the combatants will be able to adequately see each other. Safety is more important than all other considerations. If special lighting is to be used, such as a strobe light, then the combatants must be able to rehearse under that particular light source to ascertain what sort of problems they're going to encounter, and to get used to the light levels. Rehearsal under special lighting conditions must occur before the first technical rehearsal. Adjustments and changes need time. I believe the combatants and the choreographer must be able to work under the special lighting conditions at least three rehearsals prior to the first technical rehearsal.

PROPS

Any props that will be used in a fight — umbrellas, handfuls of sand, rotten fruit, canes, a woman's high-heeled shoe, bolts of cloth, a bucket of water, a spittoon — must be incorporated into rehearsals from the very beginning. Whatever the actors will handle during a fight must have top priority when acquiring props for the production. In fact it is much safer to have the attitude that any prop used in a fight should be considered a weapon and therefore potentially dangerous. It is a mistake to mime an imaginary prop during the training and rehearsal process instead of using the actual prop itself. The choreographer must stress the importance of using the actual stage prop, not a facsimile — unless an exact replica — during the entire process. This requirement is sometimes difficult to convey to a prop master who has many items to create and procure for a production, but doing so is essential. No one on the production team should take chances with the safety of an actor/combatant, least of all the fight arranger, and assuming the combatants will be able to adapt to a totally new stage prop at the last minute creates an unnecessary risk.

WEAPONS

Although outlining the use of weapons in a stage fight is not within the scope of this book, I'd like to share with you some basic principals for incorporating a knife, broken bottle, baseball bat, etc. into a hand-to-hand fight.

If at all possible avoid the use of weapons unless you have more than enough rehearsal time to carefully choreograph the sequences. Using a knife or other potentially lethal weapon is just that, potentially lethal! Be especially cautious with padding designed to absorb a knife thrust. There have been a few very tragic accounts of amateur staged fights that ended up with a young actor stabbed to death because of faulty padding. My advice is never to use padding on a combatant to deflect or absorb a real stab or thrust with a sharp object.

If you must use a weapon and the fight must be resolved by the use of that weapon, mask the actual moment of impact with a set piece or a mass of people, so that the attacker can stab far upstage of the victim and still look convincing. For further effect, create some vocal reaction, or knap, as you would for an uppercut punch. A convincing scream of agony by the victim, who then reveals a bloody, nasty wound, will often be more than sufficient for an audience.

Need I say that any knife used onstage must be ground down so that it has no cutting edge or sharp point? Sometimes it's possible to use a sharp knife prior to a fight and an identical but dull knife for the fight, thus reinforcing the illusion that a lethal weapon is being used.

Again, my advice is that the novice fight choreographer should avoid the use of weapons in a hand-to-hand fight, or hire a professional fight choreographer from the Society of American Fight Directors rather than try to work out the difficulties yourself.

I have deliberately kept this discussion to a minimum because the concerns of balance, angle of approach, handling weapon of various lengths and weights, masking, etc., are far beyond the scope of this book and will be outlined in detail in my next book on the use of weapons for the stage.

DRAMATIC THEORY

A stage fight in a well-written play is usually a dramatic visualization of an essential conflict. This central struggle may involve either basic thematic conflicts or opposition between characters. It is important, therefore, for the fight choreographer to carefully assess how the fight is to illuminate these conflicts for the audience. In other words, not only is a stage fight an opportunity to excite the audience with razzle-dazzle action, but the plot or basic character conflicts must be further illumined through the execution of the fights.

For example, in the "rape" scene between Stanley and Blanche in Tennessee

Williams's play *A Streetcar Named Desire*, the physical conflict could portray Blanche as a willing seducer who is fighting only to save face in the eyes of Stanley, who is aware of this. In this instance the choreographer would refrain from using techniques that would appear painful or demeaning, but rather would choose illusions that support the impression of rough sexual play. On the other hand, the choreographer could convey the image that Blanche is fighting for the last vestige of her self-respect and sanity, fighting with every ounce of her strength and energy. By punishing Blanche, Stanley would be pouring out all of his hate and rage for the society that treats him as an inferior. In this case the choreographer might have Stanley throw Blanche about a great deal, slap her viciously, perhaps even punch her and savagely subdue her like an animal. The fight choreographer will choose appropriate techniques to convey the espoused theories as agreed upon with the director, in order to illuminate the underlying nature of the conflict within the scene.

STYLE

In most cases the staged fight should be consistent with the style of the production as a whole. Naturally, a comedy will demand a particular style of fighting in order to evoke a humorous response, as opposed to the horror of a tragedy or the excitement of a melodrama. Sometimes it is advisable to use the fight as a counterpoint to the overall style of the production, for a special effect.

The choice of particular techniques is a major way to delineate style in stage fights. For example, a kick in the rear end would not usually be in keeping with the style of a fight in a tragedy where the major antagonist and protagonist are fighting for their lives. Pace is another way to develop a particular style in a fight. An example would be the speeded-up tempos in the comic mass fights of the Mack Sennett comedies.

Style is usually associated with particular historical periods. In the instances where style is related to historical authenticity in dress and movement patterns, it is necessary for the choreographer to research the prevalent styles of combat for the particular period in question. For example, I was asked to choreograph a fistfight in a play entitled *Childe Byron* at the Virginia Museum Theatre in Richmond. The play was set during the lifetime of Lord Byron. For this particular fight, I chose to portray the prevalent professional prizefighting techniques of that era, and I studied paintings and photographs of these fights and read accounts of them. Lord Byron actually fought in the ring on several occasions!

After practicing the fighting style myself with an assistant and videotaping the results, I was able to reproduce the movement patterns that held a flavor of the paintings and photographs of the boxers of that period, while still applying the basic principles and practices outlined in this book, to create a convincing fight. The fight adhered, of course, to the Marquis of Queensbury's rules.

CHARACTERIZATION

It would seem obvious for me to say that Muhammad Ali, Woody Allen, and Albert Einstein all fight in different ways, but the necessity for choreographers to alter the style of fighting to best portray the movement characteristics of particular characters in a play is often overlooked. It's important for the choreographer to work closely with the actors so as to be consistent with their and the director's concepts of the character's particular movement characteristics, or abilities to fight. The character in the fight scene must be consistent with the actor's portrayal throughout the production.

REHEARSAL TIME

There really can be no hard-and-fast rule governing the amount of time necessary to choreograph a given fight, because numerous factors are involved. However, I would say that the choreographer should assume that everything will take three times as long as he or she thinks it will. Some of the factors to take into consideration when bidding for adequate rehearsal time are:

1. The basic skill level of the actor/combatants. Have they been in stage fights before? Have you worked with them before?
2. Are the actors athletically inclined or not?
3. Are they quick studies?
4. Do they have phobias about violence of any sort?
5. Are they temperamental, or do they take direction well?
6. How many fights must be learned?
7. How long will the fight(s) be?
8. Will special or difficult techniques be incorporated into the fight?

It is absolutely essential that the stage fight be given priority when rehearsals are being scheduled by the director. Stage fighting is the most dangerous thing we ask actors to do, and they deserve adequate time to rehearse.

It is also essential that rehearsals be consistent as well as cumulative. A daily combat rehearsal is necessary in order to build the kinesthetic links required in learning a new movement sequence. Ample time must be taken, not only to learn the techniques, but to learn and perfect the sequence of techniques that will amount to a stage fight.

A very general rule of thumb to use when requesting rehearsal time would be an hour and a half per day every day until the show opens. Of course, if large group fights are being choreographed, then more time will be necessary. A great many directors have no idea of the needs of the fight choreographer or combatants, having never performed a fight themselves, and they may object to the amount of time taken from their rehearsal, but insist. In the long run it's much more acceptable for the actor to drop a few lines during the performance than for that actor to get a black eye or a broken nose because of an underrehearsed fight.

Another very general rule for allotting rehearsal time (when using talented performers) is that half an hour of rehearsal will be required for every five seconds of a choreographed stage fight. So a one-minute fight will require a minimum of six hours of choreographic rehearsal. Please remember that these can only be very crude estimates. Be flexible and take whatever time is necessary to ensure the safety of your performers.

REHEARSAL PROCESS

The rehearsal process should follow the procedure outlined below.

I. Conceptualization
   A. Make creative decisions after speaking with the director, designers, and actors.
   B. Write the fight down, either in longhand or using the notation system outlined later in this book.
   C. Write down a tentative rehearsal schedule for the entire rehearsal period up to the opening-night performance, and check the schedule with the director, assistant director, or stage manager.
II. Warm-up
   A. Devise a prerehearsal warm-up for the combatants, and do not fail to execute it prior to every rehearsal session.
   B. In group rehearsals, have the most physically adept combatant conduct the warm-ups, or rotate the responsibility among all the combatants.
III. Training in Fighting Techniques
   A. Train the combatants beginning with the simplest techniques first. You are developing trust between partners.
   B. Work on the most difficult techniques next, so as to give the combatants plenty of time to master them.
   C. Teach technique combinations that will be used in the actual fight so that the principles and

practices of eye contact and awareness will be instilled during transitions. Spend time on transitions and on developing convincing pain or vocal reactions.

IV. Choreography

    A. Describe the fight verbally to the combatants, so that they get some idea of what you're aiming for. Give them a general idea of what you want in relation to style and mood. Be careful not to frighten the combatants by demanding too much from them too soon. Assure them that they are very capable of executing the described fight and that you will be working quite slowly and carefully.

    B. Begin to learn and practice the most difficult combinations first. It doesn't matter whether you start at the beginning, middle, or end of the fight. There will be time to rehearse the correct sequence once the techniques and combinations have been mastered. Always work on short pieces of the routine. It is important that the fighters gain confidence by being successful and sure of themselves before moving on.

    C. Begin to link combinations and rehearse the longer sequences until they are familiar and safe. Keep the tempo slower than for the actual performance. Even if the fighters claim that they are ready to speed up, keep them under tight control. The longer they practice at a slow pace, gaining absolute control over the combination of movements, the better they will perform in the long run. Give them a copy of the notated fight and teach them how to read it, for reference and memorization.

    D. Put the entire fight together in slow motion until it is completely memorized without any lapses of memory by any of the combatants. Then, using a metronome, tamborine, etc., gradually speed up the fight to the proper performance tempos. Over a number of rehearsals, begin with slow motion, then increase to one-fourth speed, one-half speed, three-fourths speed, and performance tempo. If the fighters encounter problems with eye contact, physical control, balance, etc., stay at that tempo until they have mastered the problems. If the fight is being set to music, incorporate the accompaniment with segments of the fight as soon as full speed is reached.

E. Once the fight is at full speed, begin to fine tune it in relation to style, characterization, etc. Remember that if you change a part you will change the whole; so with each modification it is essential to repeat the whole learning process, starting very slowly. If you alter something and allow the combatants to incorporate the change too quickly, and an accident occurs, not only are you to blame, but the combatants may slide back miles in their confidence and trust.

F. Add costumes and lights, and go through the fights again, in slow motion and at one-fourth, one-half, three-fourths, and performance speeds.

G. When performing the fight for the first time for an audience, even if that audience is only the director, have the combatants perform the fight first at half speed and then at full performance tempo. This will acclimate the combatants to the new tensions that invariably result from performing.

H. Praise your combatants when they've done good work.

NOTATION

Notation systems, such as Labanotation, can be very valuable to any choreographer, if the system is thoroughly absorbed. However, I expect that the need to choreograph a fight doesn't arise very often for most of my readers, who therefore need not learn a complex notation system. I suggest a much simpler, yet effective, method to create and notate a hand-to-hand fight on paper, which may easily be taught to the actor/combatants as well. This simple method requires three basic parts: (1) narration, (2) outline, and (3) blocking.

Narration

First begin by writing out the fight as you envisage it in longhand. Here is part of my written description of a group fight I created for a production of *Arturo UI:*

Arturo UI
Gang Beating One Victim

The first attacker, A, grabs the victim by the front of his shirt and spins him into the waiting arms of two other attackers, B and C. Attacker B grabs the victim from behind by his arms, while attackers A and C, punch the victim in the stomach. C punches the victim's stomach, then A punches his stomach. The victim slumps forward, and C punches the victim's face with an uppercut, driving the victim upright. Then A punches the victim's stomach and C punches him in the groin. The victim doubles over, and B lets go from behind but continues to hold the victim's left arm. C grabs the victim's other arm, and

Table 3.1.
Outline for Fight from *Arturo UI*

	A	B	C	Victim
1.	Enters SR	Enters SR	Enters SR	Facing SL, turns around 180 degrees, to face SR
2.	Grabs victim's shirt, drags him 180 degrees clockwise, and pushes victim into the arms of B and C			
3.		Grabs victim's DS arm	Grabs victim's US arm	
4.			Releases arm and executes Stomach Punch	Reacts
5.	Stomach Punch			Reacts
6.			Uppercut Punch	Reacts
7.	Stomach Punch			Reacts
8.			Groin Punch	Reacts
9.	Lifts knee and holds leg up with both hands	Grabs victim's DS arm with both hands	Grabs victim's US arm with both hands	
10.		Flings victim forward into knee	Flings victim forward into knee	Face strikes knee; rebounds from knee and backfalls to floor
11.	Ernie Roma enters SR, strolls up to victim, performs a Groin Kick on victim, then exits SR			Reacts
12.	Exits SR	Exits SR	Exits SR	Groans and rolls on floor

together B and C throw the victim, face first, onto the waiting lifted knee of attacker A. The victim reacts by rebounding off the knee and falls to the ground on his back. Ernie Roma swaggers up and kicks the victim in the groin. All the attackers exit.

Outline

The outline of the fight will be a working blueprint for the choreographer, the combatants, and the stage manager. The stage manager will include a copy in the prompt book. Table 3.1 is an example of an outline for the same fight from *Arturo UI,* as narrated above.

Reading from the top to the bottom of the outline, you can readily ascertain the correct sequence of techniques as they occur in the fight. If any actions are written in at the same level on the page, then those actions happen simultaneously. All the details involved in the execution of the techniques are left to live training sessions and rehearsals.

Blocking

The spatial patterns created by the combatants as they move about the stage space will affect the stage "picture" and the overall impression of the fight. An added complication for the fight choreographer is that the fighters need a certain amount of stage space in order to perform their fight safely. Stage dis-

tances are strictly dictated by fighting distance between combatants and by the space requirements for particular techniques. For example, a Shoulder Roll and Layout requires a large amount of linear space. If several fighters are sharing the space, then the choreographer must time the fights so that when the roll and layout occur the space will be available. A blocking diagram will help the choreographer and the actor/combatants keep the flow patterns within the fight clear.

Figure 3.1 is an example of a blocking diagram for the same portion of the fight from *Arturo UI* that was described in writing and notated above. The number in the upper left-hand corner of each box corresponds to the number of a section in the outline. The letters within the circles correspond to those of the combatants in the outline. Arrows signify the direction of movement. The tip of the arrow indicates the point on stage where the combatant ends up. Stage right (SR) is to the left side of the box, and stage left (SL) is to the right of the box, corresponding to the performer's stage right and left. The top of the box corresponds to upstage (US), and the bottom of the box to downstage (DS).

Figure 3.2 shows some examples of broad blocking patterns that can be used when staging mass fights. Each circle with a line running through it signifies a pair of fighters.

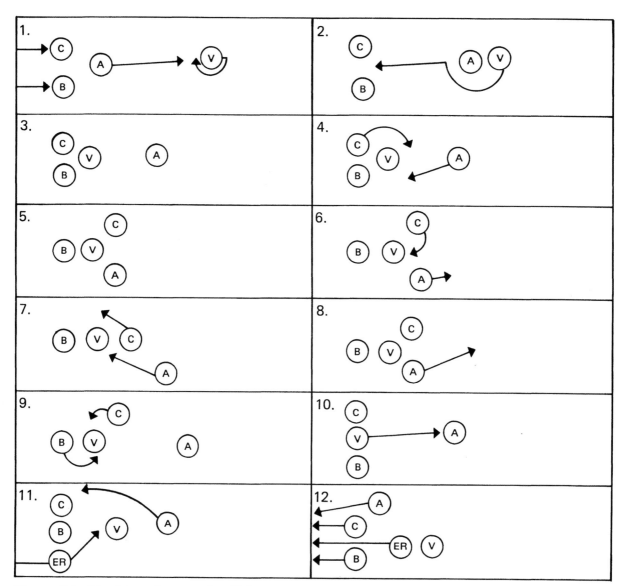

Figure 3.1. Blocking diagram for fight
from *Arturo UI*

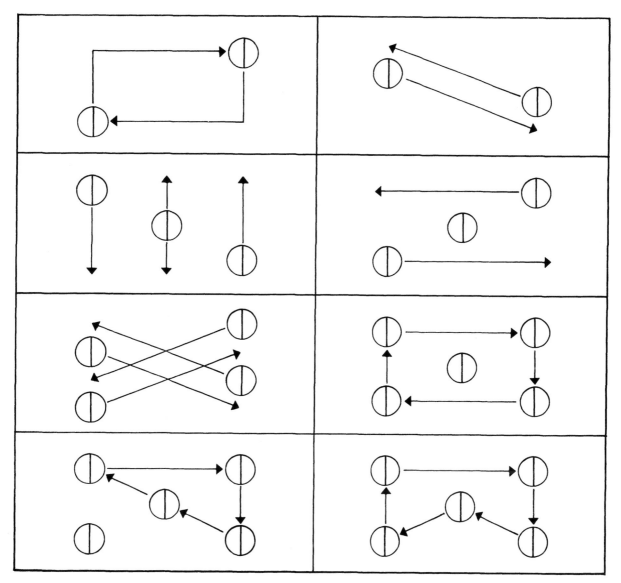

Figure 3.2 Broad blocking patterns for
mass fights

Special Effects

BLOOD RECIPES

I offer a few blood concoctions that have proven valuable to me in the past.

1. Here's a recipe that's messy but tastes pretty good!

   Mix: Chunky peanut butter

   Corn syrup

   Ketchup

   Red food coloring

2. This can be used on the face or in the mouth.

   Mix: Corn syrup

   Red food coloring

3. These mixtures are good for blood capsules.

   Mix: Glycerin

   Red food coloring

   OR

   Mix: Digestible mineral oil

   Red food coloring

4. For old fabrics, wool, sweaters, delicate fabrics (do not use on home-dyed fabrics).

   Mix: Liquid Woolite

   Red food coloring

5. For cottons, synthetics, and dyed fabrics.

   Mix: Ivory Snow laundry detergent and water, forming a thickish liquid

   Red food coloring

BLOOD BAG

Cut a corner off a plastic bag and fill the triangular plastic pouch with a blood mixture, being careful not to spill any on the outside of the bag. Fold the edges of the pack and place the edges between a folded strip of aluminum foil. Seal by pressing the foil strip with a hot iron. Attach the blood pack onto the skin with adhesive first aid tape (remember to shave body hairs), or have a pocket sewn into an undergarment if only a bloodstain is required. Break the blood pack by slapping the bag sharply. Pull at the bag as though in pain to smear the blood.

BLOOD SPONGE

A regular household sponge will absorb quite a bit of blood and hold the mixture with a relatively small amount of leakage. Merely cut a small square of sponge (or a larger sponge for more blood), moisten it, wring it out, and then soak up the blood mixture. The blood sponge can be placed in a strategic spot onstage, or in a plastic-lined pocket, to be squeezed by the actor when needed.

BLOOD BOTTLE

Acquire a small plastic bottle by purchasing antihistamine nasal spray, Elmer's Glue (particularly good because the bottle has a self-sealing cap), or contact lens solution. Remove the cap, empty the contents, rinse out the bottle, and widen the hole in the top of the cap. Fill the bottle with a dilute blood solution and replace the cap. The bottle can be kept on the actor's person with little fear of leakage until it is squeezed when needed.

BLOOD CAPSULE

Large empty gelatin capsules can be purchased from most drugstores. "Blood" made by mixing red food coloring with glycerin, corn syrup, or mineral oil is poured into one half of the capsule and capped with the other half. The capsule should be filled shortly before use, as the liquid may soften the gelatine after a short while. The blood capsule can then be carried by the actor and secretly placed into the mouth when needed. The actor merely bites down on the capsule and squeezes the contents out of the mouth for the effect.

BREAKING BONES

It is primarily the *sound* of a bone snapping that is sought when creating the illusion of breaking bones. To accomplish this, a thin piece of wood is used. Experiment with thickness; I have found anything over one-fourth inch seems unnecessary. The wood is snapped at the appropriate moment.

Acquire a thin strip of wood, approximately twelve inches long and half an inch wide, and tape the stick securely across the outside of the elbow joint with masking tape (which won't pull hairs out of the arm when removed). The tape should encircle the arm above and below the elbow joint and at each end of the strip of wood.

The wood will of course immobilize the arm at the elbow joint. When the arm is to be "broken," the attacker merely holds the victim's arm above and below the elbow, further securing the strip of wood, as the victim bends the elbow, snapping the wooden strip and creating the sound of a breaking bone. To heighten the illusion, the victim may rotate the arm at the shoulder socket so that the back of the hand faces the thigh when the elbow is bent. In this way the arm will appear to be bending in the wrong direction.

The technique of taping a strip of wood across a joint may be used on other parts of the body as well. For example, the wood may be taped across a finger joint and covered with a glove, or across a knee and covered with a pants leg.

Since we are actually seeking only the *sound* of bones breaking, either the victim or the attacker may have a strip of wood secreted in a convenient location on his or her person. For example, a long, thin pocket sewn on the inside of a trouser leg along the seam could hold a strip of wood. Then, depending upon the illusion, the victim or the attacker may create the sound of the snapping bone at the proper moment by grasping the stick with a free hand and snapping it in two. A word of caution: a broken wooden stick has jagged ends, and so the person wearing it should not move much following the breaking. The breaking of a bone should probably be choreographed as the culmination of a fight.

BREAKAWAY FURNITURE AND PROPS

It is best to start rehearsing with breakaway furniture and props early in the rehearsal process, so that the actors may get used to them. The set master or prop master can make breakaway furniture by cutting furniture apart and lightly gluing it back together again. Breakaway props such as glasses, bottles, pots, and mirrors can be bought or made from sugar, plastic, or clay.

Instructions on the construction of breakaways may be found in the following texts:

Rose, A., *Stage Effects* (New York: E.P. Dutton, 1920).

Parker, Oren W., *Scene Design and Stage Lighting* (New York: Holt, Rinehart and Winston, 1974).

Suppliers:
Alcone Company, Inc.
Paramount Theatrical Supplies
575 8th Ave.
New York, N.Y. 10018

Ben Nye
11571 Santa Monica Blvd.
Los Angeles, CA 90025

Roscoe Laboratories
36 Bush Ave.
Port Chester, N.Y. 10573

The Society of American Fight Directors
Linda McCullom, Secretary
P.O. Box 218
Blue Diamond, Nevada 89004

First Aid

MINOR INJURIES MAY arise during either rehearsal or performance of a staged fight. But the incidence of injury can be greatly reduced by using proper training processes, by paying attention to detail, and of course by using this book as a guide!

However, we all know that accidents may sometimes occur. Here is some advice on first aid for the conditions you are most likely to encounter when involved in stage fighting. I assume medical attention will be quickly sought following initial first aid! I also urge anyone who is responsible for the stage fights in a production to make every effort to enroll in a certified American Red Cross first aid training course.

BRUISES AND SWELLING

These injuries should be treated by placing an ice bag over the painful area. This limits and reduces swelling and pain.

STRAINS, SPRAINS, AND DISLOCATIONS

When such injuries occur, immobilize the body part and adjacent joints.

Strains are injuries to muscles because of overexertion. The fibers are stretched and sometimes partially torn. First aid consists of rest and warm applications, using wet towels. With a back strain the patient should lie on a hard surface such as the floor rather than on a soft surface.

Sprains, which are injuries to the soft tissues surrounding joints, usually result when the joint is forced to move beyond its normal range. The ligaments, muscle tendons, and/or blood vessels are stretched and occasionally torn or partially torn.

Swelling, tenderness, and pain on motion are the signs of a sprain. Sometimes there is discoloration of the skin over a large area because of rupture of small blood vessels. One cannot distinguish sprains from fractures by the degree of swelling and pain involved. If there is any possibility of fracture, immobilize the part as you would for a fracture (see below). Otherwise, elevate the joint upon pillows or substitutes. Applying cold, wet towels or an ice bag during the first half hour after injury may retard the swelling. Keep the joint quiet. Do not walk on a sprained ankle until it has a protective support.

A *dislocation* is a displacement of a bone end from the joint. A dislocation is usually caused by a fall or a blow. Since the signs of dislocations and fractures are similar, the person administering first aid should ordinarily handle the case as a fracture. The part should be kept quiet, and medical attention should be obtained. If the injured part is a finger or thumb, a splint is not needed if the hand is kept quiet. In the case of the shoulder, apply an arm sling to immobilize the part during transportation. It is unwise to attempt repositioning a shoulder dislocation; the result may be a long-lasting disability.

SHOCK

If there is any possibility of shock, one should seek to reduce it by keeping the victim lying down and comfortable.

Give first aid for shock to all seriously injured people. The most important evidence of shock is the victim's weakness, coupled with a skin that is pale and moist and cooler than it should be. The pulse is fast but may be weak or impossible to feel. The patient may breathe faster than usual and occasionally take deep breaths. The victim may seem alert and react optimistically but suddenly collapse.

Keep the patient lying down. This position favors the flow of blood to the head and chest, where it is needed most. If there is difficulty in breathing, the patient's head and chest should be elevated. However, elevate the lower part of the body eight to twelve inches if the blood loss has been great or the injury severe. The lower body should *not* be elevated (1) if there is a head injury, (2) if breathing difficulty is thereby increased, or (3) if the patient complains of pain as a result — for example, pain at a fracture site in the leg, or abdominal pain. For lesser injuries, such as a fracture of the wrist, elevation is unnecessary, though not harmful.

If the victim is lying on the ground or floor, place a blanket beneath him or her. Cover the patient only sparingly; the overall principle relating to heat in shock is this: Do not add heat; simply prevent a large loss of body heat.

If the patient will be under medical care within half an hour or less, the first aider need not be concerned with fluids except to allay thirst. Plain water, neither hot nor cold, is the best fluid. Stimulants such as ammonia or coffee have no value in traumatic shock.

BROKEN BONES (FRACTURES)

The objective of first aid for broken bones is to keep the broken ends and the adjacent joints quiet.

The direct evidences of fracture are swelling, tenderness to the touch, deformity, and pain on motion. Swelling requires some time to develop. The body part may be out of normal shape. You can detect deformity and swelling in doubtful cases by comparing the part with the other side of the body or with your own body. If the victim tries to move the involved body part or there is pressure or tension at the fracture site, he or she generally has pain. When completely at rest, a fractured body part usually is not painful but has a feeling of fullness or swelling. Note, however, that a person *can* move a fractured bone. Never test for fracture by having the victim move the part or attempt to walk upon a possibly broken limb.

Keep the broken ends quiet. Keep the adjacent joints quiet. Give first aid for shock. Seek medical aid.

If the fracture is compound (the bone breaks the skin), apply a sterile dressing to the wound. Control the bleeding by direct pressure. If splints are to be applied in cases where bleeding has been severe, leave a tourniquet loosely in place above the wound so that if bleeding resumes it can quickly be controlled. Do not push a protruding bone back in place.

Fractures should be treated with an ice bag over the painful area. This limits and reduces swelling and pain.

Partial immobilization of the extremity bones may be attained by placing them on pillows.

HEAD INJURIES

The objective in first aid for a head injury is to keep the person quiet.

If the patient is unconscious, place a small pillow or a substitute under the head. Turn the head toward the side so that secretions may drool from the corner of the mouth. Loosen clothing about the neck. If the patient is awake, he or she may lie flat.

Whether the victim is conscious or not, give no stimulants.

If a dressing is needed for a scalp wound, merely lay a large dressing over the injury and then apply a full head bandage.

"BLACK EYES"

Bruises of the soft tissue beneath the eye often involve rupture of small blood vessels. Color changes then occur over several days, causing the familiar "black eye." Immediate cold applications tend to halt the bleeding and prevent some of the swelling. Later the application of warm wet towels will hasten absorption of the discoloring substances.

CUTS AND ABRASIONS

The objectives in treating a cut or abrasion are to protect the wound from contamination and control bleeding.

For small cuts, merely wash the area thoroughly and apply pressure directly over the wound with a clean cloth.

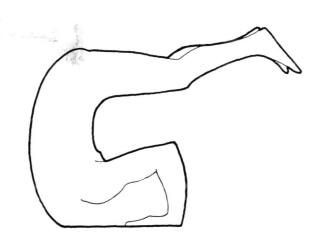

Index